Fred Morrow Fling

Greek and Roman Civilization

With an Introduction to the Source Study Method

Fred Morrow Fling

Greek and Roman Civilization
With an Introduction to the Source Study Method

ISBN/EAN: 9783337009021

Printed in Europe, USA, Canada, Australia, Japan

Cover: Foto ©ninafisch / pixelio.de

More available books at **www.hansebooks.com**

STUDIES

IN

EUROPEAN HISTORY

GREEK AND ROMAN CIVILIZATION

WITH AN INTRODUCTION TO THE SOURCE
STUDY METHOD

BY
FRED MORROW FLING, Ph.D.
The University of Nebraska

SECOND EDITION

LINCOLN, NEBRASKA
J. H. MILLER
1899

CONTENTS.

	PAGE
Introduction	v
I. The Homeric Age	1-15
II. The Athenian Constitution	17-29
III. Spartan Life	31-44
IV. Alexander's Methods of Warfare	47-62
V. The Achaean League	63-75
VI. The Roman Constitution	77-92
VII. Roman Life of the First Punic War	93-108
VIII. Roman Life of the Jugurthine Period	109-124
IX. Roman Life Under the Empire	125-144
X. Roman Law	145-163

INTRODUCTION.

The pedagogy of the last half of the nineteenth century differs both in matter and in method from that of the first half. Our age is scientific above all things, and this spirit has permeated, one by one, all branches of instruction. The change in matter has consisted in a revolt against the claims of the classics to a monopoly of all knowledge and all discipline. The revolt was successful and the classics were relegated to their proper place in the new curriculum. Henceforth they are to form a part and not the whole of education. Through the breach thus made new studies entered demanding their share of attention. In truth, some of them demanded more than their share, and for a time, under the influence of the reactionary spirit, the movement threatened to go too far in the opposite direction and to abandon the classics entirely.

But the new matter was not more important than the new method. With the sciences came the scientific spirit and the laboratory method. The old method, or lack of method, presided at the birth of the new studies, but the text-book recitation was at first supplemented by experiments performed before the class, and at last by experiments performed by the class, and the change was complete. That the laboratory method was the only method to be employed in teaching the sciences was quite clear; that it had a universal application and might be as readily employed in teaching other subjects, not generally recognized as sciences, was not so clear. The result of this apparent inability to understand the great possibilities in the new method has been a marked absence of progress in the teaching of certain subjects. History, unfortunately, is one of these. I say "unfortunately," for I know of no subject whose right teaching is of more importance, especially for the people of a democracy. And yet it was but natural that history should be one of the last subjects to feel the touch of the scientific influence. Its subject was commonplace—humanity; its material—the every day objects found under the hands and eyes of every human being. Neither subject nor material lent itself readily to scientific treatment. The impulse to change generally comes from the top and it was only in the last generation that the historical method was sufficiently developed to make it possible for the great teachers of history to give that impulse. But at last the impulse has been given and is making its way through our whole system. Up to the present time, however, it has made the greatest progress in the universities and better colleges and has not produced a very deep impression upon the secondary schools. Yet the signs are not lacking to prove that the time has come for energetic and systematic work in the grades below the college. As an aid to this work, the following "source" extracts have been prepared, with an introduction upon method and its application in the secondary schools.

A good definition of history is not easy to find, but perhaps one of the best is that given by Bernheim: "History is the science of the evolution of man in his activities as a social being." Let us examine the definition carefully and endeavor to get at its meaning. In the first place, it is claimed that history is a science, that is, a body of systematized knowledge. If, as has been recently affirmed, there is no science but exact science and natural science, and man is excluded from the realm of nature, our claim cannot be allowed. But I am inclined to think that all sciences are not equally exact, and that if the term "natural" be used to exclude man, then there are sciences that are not natural sciences. I am also inclined to think that man is as natural as any other animal. The refusal to concede to history a place among the sciences may have had some weight a hundred years ago, but it has none to-day. "Knowledge is science in the degree in which it can be subjected to method and law and so rendered comprehensible and certain. Under this test history must surely be assigned the rank of a science, though confessedly inexact and as yet but partially wrought out." But what science is absolutely exact or completely wrought out? All are in a state of flux, and are more or less inexact and incomplete. History is one of the late comers. Its greater incompleteness and inexactness as a science are due to its complexity and to the fact that its development depends so largely upon the development of a considerable number of auxiliary sciences.

We note in the second place that history is the "science of the evolution of man." History is no longer a simple teller of stories; the muse has set herself a sterner task. We are conscious that the society of to-day differs from the society of one thousand years ago. An evolution has taken place and it is the work of the historian to trace this evolution through all its phases. It should be noted, further, that it is not simply the evolution of the American, nor of the Englishman, but the evolution of all men. This idea is too new to be fully realized, but in the period of African, Chinese, and Japanese wars, it should be evident to the most superficial observer that history, universal history, has for its theater the whole globe and for its actors all mankind.

The last point in the definition to be considered is the fact that history has to do with *all* the activities of man as a social being. History is not simply "past politics." It is that and something more, for in order to understand the meaning of the social evolution of man, all the expressions of man's life in society must be considered, whether these expressions be political, economic, literary, artistic, or religious. It is with man's social life in its completeness that the historian has to do.

The historian then attempts to describe the evolution of the society of which he himself forms a part. But how can this evolution be traced? The old Greeks, Romans, and Germans, are long since dead and cannot be called back to life that we may study their civilization. That civilization must be reconstructed, but how and from what material? Shall we allow full play to our imaginations and call the result an historical reconstruction? Such a history would have as much value as the work of a botanist who had never studied plant life. There is but one way to reconstruct the life of the past and that is from the remains of the past. Everything that has come down from the past must be used in reconstructing the past. These remains are called historical sources. As the word "history" is applied indiscriminately to both the fact and the record of the fact, it is of the utmost importance that, at the very outset, we draw the line sharply between the two. The historical fact is what actually did happen in all its fullness and truthfulness; the record of the fact is the belief of certain persons as to what happened. It is self-evident that the fact and the record of the fact may be quite different things. In truth, they generally are quite different and never can be exactly the same. If this last assertion be correct, then we can never know exactly what happened at a certain time and in a certain place and it is evident that absolute historical truth is beyond our reach.

An examination of the way in which the record is made will make more clear the truth of the above statement. An event takes place and is gone. One or more persons make a record of it. Our knowledge of the event is obtained from the record. If it be inexact or incomplete we are helpless, for the event will not take place again. It cannot be conjured up a second time and induced to move slowly that we may catch its slightest peculiarity. The botanist, the chemist, and the physicist may repeat their experiments until the record is satisfactory, while the historian is often dependent upon the record of an event made by a careless or ignorant observer. What we have before us then is not a photograph of the fact, for the fact passed through a human brain before reaching paper and was more or less distorted in the passage. A hundred and one things may conspire to make this record defective. Physical defects, combined with ignorance, passion, and prejudice may so transform the fact as to render it hardly recognizable and to make the record a veritable caricature. And when, in addition to all this, the record is not made upon the spot, time plays strange tricks with the memory and renders the transformation even greater. Such are the difficulties of making the fact, or that which actually happened, agree with the record of the fact, or the belief as to what happened. What actually happened is called objective history; what is believed to have happened is called subjective history. The aim of the scientific historian is to make the last approximate as closely as possible to the first. This can be done only by a most exhaustive collection of all the records and remains relating to the event and a most careful and critical examination and interpretation of them. But what specifically are these sources? They are the records of eye and ear witnesses; of the persons taking part in the event or present when the event took place; all direct remains from the event that have come down to us and enable us to form a setting for the event. In the case of a battle, we search for the diaries and letters of the combatants; we interrogate survivors; we read the dispatches of generals and the reports of observers; we study the battle-field, the arms and equipments, and the resources of either side. In short, all material is collected that can throw any light upon the event itself and help us to restore it. The sources may be classified as follows:

I. Historical remains.
    A. In narrow sense.
        a. Remains of men.
        b. Languages.
        c. Social conditions: manners and customs, festivals, forms of worship, institutions, laws, constitutions.
        d. Products of human skill: utensils, arms, buildings, coins.

  c. Records: courts, assemblies, speeches, newspapers, letters, tax-rolls, etc.
 B. In broader sense.
  a. Monuments.
  b. Inscriptions.
II. Traditions.
 A. Pictorial: statutory, pictures.
 B. Oral: stories, anecdotes, songs.
 C. Written: annals, chronicles, biographies.

While the reconstruction of a period in history must rest upon the historical sources coming down to us, much help in interpretation of the sources is obtained from analogy. There exist to-day upon the globe societies representing many of the stages through which our civilization has passed. Through the study of existing societies much light is cast upon the obscure places in past development.

These sources then, the remains of the event itself, and the descriptions of it, are the material with which the historian must work. The difference between the sources and a narrative text must be fully grasped before the new method can be understood. Grote's History of Greece is not a source, but the result of Grote's study of the sources, his attempt to reconstruct the past from the sources. The value of this reconstruction is determined by comparing it with the sources, and the sources of Greek history are all the things enumerated above under the heads of Historical Remains and Traditions. Where are these sources enumerated? First of all in bibliographies devoted to the histories of particular countries. In some of the older bibliographies no distinction is made between sources and modern writers, but in the latest scientific works the two classes are kept separate. When a work on bibliography is not accessible, the information may be obtained from the foot-notes of a modern historical narrative. Turn to a volume of Gibbon or Macaulay and at the bottom of each page will be found an enumeration of the sources of information. From these footnotes a complete list of Gibbon's or Macaulay's sources may be obtained.

But when the historian has collected his material, he has only taken the first step. The material must be tested and its value determined. Upon the success of this criticism of the sources depends the value of the reconstruction. What will be its value if it rests upon worthless material? We must know first of all if the material is genuine, that is, if it is what it pretends to be. Much material that the last century accepted as genuine has been rejected as false by this, and often as intentionally false, or forged. The "Forged Decretals" and "The Gift of Constantine" are but two of many examples that might be cited. I have not space to enumerate the tests by which evidence is tried to determine its genuineness. In spite of the high degree of development attained in this branch of historical method, the results reached are not always satisfactory. The different opinions among specialists touching the lately discovered "Athenian Constitution," of Aristotle, is a not uncommon illustration of inability to reach satisfactory results.

If our material has stood the tests of genuineness, we then proceed to consider its relation to the event. Suppose, for example, we have a description of the battle of Salamis; what do we want to know about that account in order to determine its value? First of all, who wrote it? Herodotus. Who was Herodotus? A Greek. Was he living at the time?

Probably. Was he present at the battle? Probably not. Why not? The battle took place in 480 B. C. and Herodotus was born about 485 B. C. That would make him about five years old at the time. It is evident, then, that Herodotus, although he lived at the time, could not have been present at the battle and must have obtained his information from others and many years later. He is not, then, a source, but was obliged to write his account from the sources, as a man born in 1860 might write the history of our Civil War. This conclusion is both true and false. There are cases in which a work that was not originally a source might become a source, namely, when all the material upon which that work is based has been lost. The sources with which Herodotus worked have disappeared and we cannot go back of him. He is practically our court of final appeal. Having now decided that the account of the battle of Salamis in Herodotus is the principal source of information, shall we proceed at once to use it? That is, is the criticism at an end, and is it time to reconstruct the event from the record? Not yet. We want to know more about this man and the conditions under which he wrote. What had been his education, what was his position in society, what his special preparation for writing? In a word, was he able to tell the truth? But a man may be able to tell the truth and not be willing to do so. Herodotus lived in Asia Minor. Was he friendly to the Persians and hostile to the Greeks? Was he an aristocrat? He might be unfair to the Athenians. Was he a democrat? He might be unjust toward the Spartans. How can these questions be answered? By a careful study of the work of Herodotus, page by page, and line by line, aided in the study by opinions of men like Grote, Curtis, and other historians of Greece who have covered the same ground. The tests thus applied might be summed up under the following heads:

LOCALIZATION.

I. Who was the writer?
II. When was the work written?
III. Where was it written?

VALUE OF EVIDENCE.

IV. Was he able to tell the truth?
V. Was he willing to tell the truth?

It is easily seen that question V. is the least easily and satisfactorily answered. A negative answer to this question would have the most disastrous effect. The absolute conviction on the part of the historian that his witness was not truthful would lead him to reject the evidence. The reconstruction of the event might have produced far different results had the evidence been accepted. It often happens that the different versions of an event found in different historians is due to the fact that one historian believes a certain witness honest and the other believes him dishonest.

The work of criticism being ended, the work of reconstruction begins.

The first step in reconstruction is the establishment of the facts. The event may be described by a single witness, by several witnesses that agree in substance, or by several witnesses that disagree. In the first case the value of the evidence will depend upon the general character of the witness and the way in which his evidence harmonizes with our general knowledge of the period; the second case represents the most satisfactory kind of evidence, when the witnesses are independent of one another. In the last case, the evidence of the most reliable witnesses must be set over against the least reliable, and when they disagree the evidence of the unreliable witnesses is rejected. These are the general principles. I have not space to point out in what manner they are modified in the application.

Having established the individual facts, the next step is to arrange them. This may be done under the heads of time and place, that is, we may arrange in their order all the events that have taken place in the United States (place) during the nineteenth century (time), or it may be done in accordance with the relation of the facts to some feature of the history of the period studied, as the constitution, the religion, the art, etc. The two methods may, of course, be combined, that is, we may arrange the facts with regard to religion in the United States, in the nineteenth century. The arrangement of the facts is determined by the object that the historian has in mind and is nothing more than putting his notes in order that he may see what they mean as a whole, and what the development has been. At first sight it might appear that the work of reconstruction was now at an end. But this is far from the truth.

The facts having been established it is necessary to determine what each fact means (interpretation) and what they all mean when taken together (combination). The interpretation of the sources is divided into interpretation of the remains, of the traditions, and interpretation of the sources by one another. Suppose that we have established the fact that in one of the European countries milestones of a certain kind and the remains of walls of a peculiar construction are encountered along the roads. Interpretation justifies us in saying that this was once the course of a Roman highway. This is the simplest form of interpretation of remains. More difficult problems in interpretation would be to restore the coinage system of a country from the coins that remained, or to describe the condition of the early European tribes from the root words common to all the Aryan people on the continent. An interpretation of the facts of tradition demands a knowledge of the writing of the period we are studying, of the style of the writer, of the time and place where the record originated, and the character of the writer. All of these things have been mentioned under the head of general criticism; they must be applied in the interpretation of each fact, for if we do not understand all these things, we shall fail to interpret the facts correctly. Last of all, we are much aided in the work of reconstruction, through the interpretation of the sources by one another. The documents are often unintelligible, and the contemporary narrative written by those who have helped to make the documents tell us what they mean. The Iliad and the Odyssey are used to interpret the remains found in Greece and in Asia Minor. Having now fixed the facts and interpreted them it is necessary to combine these interpretations that we may get a view of the whole subject. The combined result must be lighted up by phantasy that working upon the results given it by criticism, interpretation, and combination endeavors to see the events in the form in which they happened. It is not with the imagination playing freely that we have to do here, but with the phantasy dealing with definite data. Where the phantasy is defective the highest results are not obtained; where the imagination is uncontrolled, the results are unscientific and often worthless. Phantasy, as here used, means the ability to restore the historical past from definite data without doing violence to the data. But all the difficulties of reproduction have not yet been enumerated.

The final conception of the subject calls for an understanding of the physical, psychical, and social conditions under which the events took place and their relation to other events. For the factors to be considered in dealing with human development are the influences of nature, the psychology of the individual and of the masses, and the institutions under which the individual lives. Geography, psychology, and sociology are for the student of history, auxiliary sciences. Last of all, in considering the subject, treated in its deepest and broadest meaning, the historian rises into the realm of the philosophy of history.

Having thus, step by step, proceeding from the most particular to the most general, formed a conception of the past period in accord with the evidence, the historian commits it to paper, supporting his narrative throughout by proof. His work is done. He has worked carefully, faithfully, and honestly, but it must not be forgotten that the value of the result depends upon the ability of the historian and the material at his disposal. If he had at his disposal all the sources in existence, if criticisms, interpretations, combinations, and reproductions were infallible, it would never be necessary to rewrite the history of that period. But that is inconceivable and as a consequence *history is constantly being rewritten from the sources.*

Such is the way in which history is written.

"But why," you ask, "has so much space been devoted to the way in which history is written? I want to know how to study history and how to teach it." The student of history and the teacher of history must learn of the writer of history. His method must be our method. This position is sound and is in harmony with the scientific spirit that characterizes all our school work to-day. You may *read* history, if you will, but do not imagine that you are *studying* history, if you are not employing the method of the historian working directly with the sources and forming your own judgment.

The objection will be raised that this might do for the specialist in history, but is out of place when applied to all students of history. But this argument is not logical. It is just as necessary that all students of history should do laboratory work in history by going to the sources, as that all students of botany, chemistry, and physics should do laboratory work in those lines. As I have already said, the laboratory idea is more novel when applied to history than when applied to some other subjects, but it is not less true because it is novel. It is not the intention to make historians of all our boys and girls, but rather to teach them to study what history they do study scientifically. And it is high time that this work were being done. For if there is any one thing that we need more than another in our political life, it is men who are capable of determining what are facts and of telling what those facts mean. In the past, history has been read and recited in our schools that our boys and girls might obtain a certain amount of information concerning their nation or their race. May it be studied in the future for the further purpose of disciplining their minds and rendering them capable of forming sound, independent judgments upon the sources or the raw materials of history! To such a mind the opinion of another is of value only as far as it rests upon evidence that stands unscathed the test of the severest criticism.

Having considered the way in which history is written, it is now in order to point out its application in teaching. The success of the application in the schoolroom will depend upon the extent to which the teacher is filled with the spirit of historical research. To acquire a fair share of this spirit, genius is not necessary, but simply a desire to know the truth and a willingness to search patiently for it. I shall assume, then, that the teacher possesses some of the spirit that she wishes to impart to her pupils, and that she is endeavoring to develop more of that spirit in herself.

It might be possible to deal with the application of the method to all the grades, from the primary to the graduate courses in the university, but that would be too comprehensive and would pass beyond the scope of this chapter. It is not the intention to describe an ideal state of things, but to take the teaching of history as it exists and to show how it may be improved. We shall consider, then, how the study of the sources may be made practical for the high schools, and how by devoting no more time to the teaching of the subject than is now given, better results may be obtained.

The source work cannot be done without a collection of sources any more than botany can be studied without plants. But by a collection of sources I do not mean a library; I mean a book made up of extracts from the sources and photographs of the historical remains. This book must be placed in the hands of the pupil. I have talked with teachers who told me that they were "using the new method," and I have discovered that there was but one copy of a book of sources in the schoolroom, and that was on the teacher's desk. They believed that they were using the new method, but I fear that they did not know what the new method is.

The book of sources is not a narrative like the ordinary school history. It does not read smoothly. "It seems to be disconnected," as one puzzled teacher put it. She was right. It is disconnected, and it is the duty of the pupil under the guidance of the teacher to connect it. Out of the photographs of ruins, of temples, of statuary, of remains of every kind, out of the extracts from documents, diaries, contemporary narratives, newspapers, etc., this brick and lumber and mortar of history— teacher and pupil are to do on a small scale what the historian does upon a large scale— reconstruct the past.

The narrative school history — Myers, Barnes, or Swinton—can never take the place of the book of sources, nor can the book of sources take the place of the narrative. *The pupils should use both. If they can have but one, it should be the book of sources, supplemented by a condensed statement of connecting facts.* The narrative text and the book of sources supplement one another. The book of sources contains the material *to be worked up into a narrative;* the other book *contains the material that has been worked up into a narrative.* This comparison of the book of sources with a good narrative text should be continued until their relation is understood. The books are not opposed to one another, but *they are not the same thing and one cannot do the work of the other.*

The source extracts that follow may be used in various ways. They may be employed simply as supplementary reading in connection with a narrative history; they may be used to supplement a book made up partly of sources—like the Sheldon-Barnes histories,—not all of the questions being answered, or each study may be worked over thoroughly in accordance with the directions that follow. In that case, one or two hours a week would be devoted to the topic until the study upon it was complete. This is one of the most conservative ways of introducing source study. The remaining hours of the week could be devoted to the continuous study of some portion of European History. This book of source extracts should not be confounded with the books, sometimes called source books, that contain source extracts plus a condensed statement of connecting facts. Such a book may furnish material enough for a connected study of European History; the extracts in this book do not.

The work begins by an examination of the book of extracts that the pupil may understand what they are and what he is to do with them. The method of work should then be explained and for the morrow's lesson a number of questions upon the first extract assigned for preparation. The mistake of requiring too much work at the outset should not be made. Many of the questions look simple to the teacher; they may not appear so simple to the pupil. Moreover, if the teacher be a bright woman, she will not limit herself, in the class discussion, to these questions, but will add others suggested by her own study.

Before the pupils come into the class, they must prepare their lesson. This lesson consists in answering a number of questions, or, in other words, solving a number of problems. This is the rock upon which a large majority of the teachers have been wrecked. They did not insist upon the preparation and the work was not done. Each question must be answered fully, the answers written neatly in a note-book and brought into the class in that form. This should represent the independent thought of the pupil and should enable one to gauge his ability. An answer that does not carry its proof with it should not be accepted. "Yes" and "No" are not complete answers; they are simply theorems to be demonstrated. "Why did you answer 'yes'?" is the question to be put at once, and the pupil must understand that his work is not finished until he has *proved his point by evidence taken from his source-book*. This reasoning must all appear in the answer contained in the note-book.

When the class meets each pupil has before him, *open on the desk*, his note-book with answers and his source-book. This exercise is not to be a test of memory. The teacher should not waste the recitation hour in trying to discover how many facts have lodged in the brain of this boy or of that girl. Let the teacher read the first question and call for an answer. She should be sure the answer is *read*. Boys and girls have an innate objection to doing things in the right way. She told them to write the answers out, but some of them did not think she meant it. She must convince them that they are unprepared if they come to class without the written answer. The answer read, she proceeds to criticise it. First of all, has any evidence been omitted? Let other members of the class supply it. Is the reasoning incorrect? She forces the pupil to defend his answer with the evidence before him and follows him from point to point until he sees that it cannot be defended. When his conclusions are wrong, she does not tell him so at once and give him the right answer, but lets him see that he has not proved his point. It may be through lack of evidence; it may be from a false interpretation or combination. The whole discussion plays around this pupil's answer, and the rest of the class is drawn into it. The pupils having more evidence and other conclusions contribute them. While this discussion is going on, every member of the class follows closely and takes down in his note-book every bit of evidence that he had overlooked and every interpretation or combination that he had not noticed in writing his answers. At the close of the hour each pupil goes away knowing more about the subject than when he came. He carried in his own work; in the class room he added the ideas of the teacher and of fellow pupils. The class notes, as proof of attention, must be insisted upon and kept distinct from the original answers.

The work goes on in this manner until all the questions on the topic have been answered and discussed. Many teachers have thought that the work stopped here, but if the method of the historian is to be our model, that cannot be true. We must arrange and classify our results and see how they look as a whole. The results to be arranged are the answers and class notes. Let this be explained to the pupils and let it be pointed out that their work on the topic will be finished only when the judgments they have formed are arranged in the shape of a narrative. They should be told that they are writing history. It may not be very valuable history for the world at large, but it may be very valuable for them. Their conclusions may be very weak, but it is only through the exercise of the judgment that they learn to draw sound conclusions. They are to analyze their results and this analysis is to be given the form of an outline. If they do not know how to make an outline, time should be taken to teach them. The material should not be arranged for them, but an outline of some subject should be upon the board showing them how to make heads and sub-heads. Then they should be allowed to try their hands on their own material.

These outlines—or some of them—should be placed on the board before the recitation and criticised during the recitation. The attempt should not be made to run them all in one mould, but the pupils should know what they are about and be able to give reasons for their divisions and subdivisions. Above all, no points should appear in the outline that cannot be supported by evidence. It is true that—as a student once remarked—"a man has a right to his opinion," but it is equally true that in history that opinion is of no value unless it rests on evidence.

The last step consists in composing a short narrative, based upon and following the outline closely. Portions of these narratives should be read and criticised, and some especially good narrative read in its entirety in the class. Here, as elsewhere, the teacher should watch closely for unsound general statements, for inexact and incomplete statements. Any and all of these things indicate that the pupil is not working with his eye on the evidence. The reading of the narrative completes the study on that topic, and the same operation is repeated with the next topic.

As the pupil goes from topic to topic and handles one bit of evidence after another, the teacher should let slip no opportunity of acquainting him with the principles of the historic method in their simplest forms. By the use of many simple illustrations, and by frequent reiteration, the boy or girl is led to see something of the value of the study of the life of humanity and to understand something about his relation to it. He may learn, little by little, that the restoration of the past must rest upon evidence, and after he has made an intelligent study of a period, he should be able to enumerate the evidence used. In connection with his American history he might even be allowed to collect evidence and to learn something of its value. Pupils may be sent to old residents to gather information touching the history of the town, state, or nation. They may be asked to make a list of the sources that would be used in writing a history of the town. This list should be based upon their personal research. Of course, with young pupils the matter of criticism cannot be carried far, but they can learn that an eye and ear witness is the best kind of a witness. The boy who *went* to the circus is listened to in preference to the boy who did not go, but has *heard* about it. They can understand why we should go to the diary of Columbus if we want to know what happened on his voyage to America. They can even understand why the evidence of one witness is better than that of another. They know that if their father belongs to one political party he does not believe what the papers of the other party say. It would also be an easy matter to show how difficult it is to learn the whole truth about an event. They may write independent accounts of something that has recently taken place in the city or town, and of which they have personal knowledge. The accounts should be as careful and detailed as possible. Let them compare the accounts, noting the different points of view and attempting to reconcile them, thus establishing the matter of fact. In this way in the work in United States or general history a thousand opportunities will occur to familiarize the pupils with the principles of the historical method. There should be but little generalization at the outset; the generalizations should develop naturally from the specific cases.

It should be said by way of anticipation, that the teacher should not feel discouraged if she does not get on rapidly at first. Let her have patience and persevere; let her remember that the principles of historical criticism are but the rules of common sense employed in every day life, and she will soon see light.

The success of the work will depend, to a large extent, upon the control of the note-book. I have found that the most satisfactory book is one with a separable cover. The leaves are tied in as fast as needed. Covers and paper may be obtained at a very small cost. The material should be arranged in the book in an orderly manner. My system has been to follow this order: Answers, Class Notes, Outlines, Narratives. A heading on each sheet indicated the topic to which the answers belonged and all the answers were numbered. Sheets of brown cardboard separated the Answers from the Class notes, the Class notes from the Outlines, etc. The object of all this system was to render the examination of the books easy. For they must be examined at fixed intervals and a record kept of their condition. The work will not succeed unless the pupil does his duty and the condition of his book is an excellent test of how he is doing it. The record for each pupil may be kept upon a separate sheet, with the following columns, running from left to right: Due (when the book was due and when handed in), Answers (how many, quantity, and quality), Class notes (quantity and quality), Outline, Narrative, Oral Discussion (part taken by the pupil in class discussion). At the end of the term the card will give a good idea of what the pupil has done. There was one other column headed "Time" and in it was noted the number of hours given to the preparation of lessons. It was taken from the student's "time card," kept in the back of his note-book. This "time card" was of the size of the note-book and was ruled with columns at the left for the date, in the center for a statement of the work done (writing answers, making outlines, etc.), and at the right for the hours or minutes given to the work. The keeping of this card is a valuable piece of work in itself. Such are the general suggestions touching the work. Others will be made from time to time throughout the year.

The following works contain about everything that exists on method in the English language. They have to do more with the question of how to study history than how to teach it, but I have tried to show that the teacher must know how to study history before she can teach it. These are books that every teacher of history, who is not a teacher simply for a year and a day, should possess. They should form the beginning of a professional library. Study them, meditate upon them, and apply their teachings. Go to them again and again, until you have mastered them and are ready for something better:

Freeman, E. A., Methods of Historical Study, London, 1886; Droysen, J. G., Principles of History, Boston, 1893; Hall, G. S., Methods of Teaching History, Boston, 1889; Andrews, E. B., Brief Institutes of General History, Boston, 1890; Arnold, T., Modern History, New York, 1895; Acton, Lord, The Study of History, London, 1896; Stubbs, W., Medieval and Modern History, Oxford, 1887; Barnes, M. S., Studies in Historical Method, Boston, 1896; Hinsdale, B. A., How to Study and Teach History, N. Y., 1895; Langlois, Ch. V., and Seignobos, Ch.: Introduction to the Study of History, N. Y., 1898; Fling, F. M., Outline of Historical Method, Lincoln, 1899.

THE HOMERIC AGE.

CHAPTER I.

THE HOMERIC AGE.

HOMER probably never lived, and the Iliad is evidently a national product, not composed by one man at one time, but by many men at different times. As a record of the Trojan War, the poem has practically no value. Its real value to the student of history is due to the fact that it unconsciously reveals to us the manners and customs of the age in which it was composed. While the imagination may construct wholes that are not real, the real elements with which the poet or novelist works are drawn from experience. It is possible, then, for the historian to sift out these elements and make use of them. The procedure is psychologically sound, and its value may be easily tested. While none of the events of Mr. Howell's novels, for example, are necessarily true, the historian could draw from many of them true descriptions of the life of New England in the nineteenth century.

What is true of the literature of this century is even truer of the literature of past centuries. The old bards could not construct their imaginary pictures of the earlier society without making use of the elements found in the society of which they themselves formed a part.

I. THE HOMERIC AGE.

> Lang, Leaf, Myers: The Iliad of Homer. Macmillan & Co., New York, 1889.

A. *Government.*

> The folk began to perish, because Atreides had done dishonor to Chryses, the priest. For he had come to the

Achaians' fleet ships to win his daughter's freedom, and brought a ranson beyond telling; . . . and made his prayer unto all the Achaians and most of all to the two sons of Atreus, orderers of the host: "Ye sons of Atreus and all ye well-grieved Achaians, now may the Gods that dwell in the mansions of Olympus grant you to lay waste the city of Priam and to fare happily homeward; only set ye my dear child free, and accept the ransom." . . . Then all the other Achaians cried assent to reverence the priest and accepted his goodly ransom; yet the thing pleased not the heart of Agamemnon, son of Atreus, but he roughly sent him away. (Pages 1, 2.)

"Nor do thou, son of Peleus, think to strive with a king, might against might: seeing that no common honor pertaineth to a sceptered king, to whom Zeus apportioneth glory. Though thou be strong . . . yet his is the greater place, for he is king over more." (Page 10.) Then woke he (Agamemnon) from sleep, and the heavenly voice was in his ears. So he rose up sitting, and donned his soft tunic, fair and bright, and cast around him his great cloak, and beneath his glistering feet he bound his fair sandals, and over his shoulder cast his silver studded sword, and grasped his sire's sceptre, imperishable forever, wherewith he took his way amid the mail-clad Achaians' ships. (Page 22.)

Now went the goddess, Dawn, to high Olympus, foretelling daylight to Zeus and all the immortals; and the king bad the clear voiced heralds summon to the assembly the flowing haired Achaians. So did those summon and these gathered with speed.

But first the council of the great hearted elders met beside the ship of King Nestor the Pylos-born. And he that had assembled them framed his cunning council: "Hearken, my friends. A dream from heaven came to me in my sleep through the ambrosial night. . . . So spake the dream and was flown away, and sweet sleep left me. So come, let us now call to arms as we may the sons of the Achaians. But first I will speak to make trial of them as is fitting, and will bid them flee with their benched ships; only do ye from this side and from that seek to hold them back."

So spake he and sat him down; and there stood up among them Nestor who was king of sandy Pylos. He of good intent made harangue to them. . . . So spake he and led the way forth from the council and all the other sceptered chiefs rose with him and obeyed the shepherd of the host; and the people hastened to them. . . . From ships and huts, before the low beach, marched forth their many tribes and companies to the place of assembly. . . . And the place of assembly was in an uproar, and the earth echoed again as the hosts sat them down, and there was turmoil. Nine heralds restrained them with shouting, if perchance they might refrain from clamor and harken to their kings. And hardly at the last would the people sit and keep them to their benches and cease from noise. Then stood up Lord Agamemnon, bearing his scepter. . . . Thereon he leaned and spake his saying to the Argives. (Pages 22-24.)

So said she, and he knew the voice of the goddess speaking to him and set him to run, and cast away his mantle the which his herald gathered up . . . that waited on him. And himself he went to meet Agamemnon, son of Atreus, and at his hand received the septre of his sires, imperishable forever, wherewith he took his way amid the ships of the mail-clad Achaians.

Whenever he found one that was a captain and a man of mark, he stood by his side, and refrained him with gentle words: "Good sir, it is not seemly to affright thee like a coward, but do thou sit thyself, and make all thy folk sit down. For thou knowest not yet clearly what is the purpose of Atreus' son. . . . And we heard not all of us what he spake in the council. Beware lest in his anger he evilly entreat the sons of the Achaians." . . . But whatever man of the people he saw and found him shouting, him he drave with his sceptre and chode with loud words: "Good sir, sit still, and harken to the words of others that are thy betters; but thou art no warrior and a weakling, never reckoned whether in battle or in council. In no wise can we Achaians all be kings here. A multitude of masters is no good thing; let there be one master, one king, to whom the son of crooked counseling Cronos had granted it, even the sceptre and the judgments that he may rule among you." (Page 27.)

Now all the rest sat down and kept their place upon the benches. Only Thersites still chattered on, the uncontrolled of speech, whose mind was full of words, many and disorderly, wherewith to strive against the chiefs idly and in no good order, but even as he deemed that he should make the Argives laugh. And he was ill favored beyond all men that came to Ilios. Bandy-legged was he and lame of one foot, and his two shoulders rounded, arched down upon his chest; and over them his head was warped and a scanty stubble

THE HOMERIC AGE.

sprouted on it. Hateful was he to Achilles above all and to Odysseus, for them he was wont to revile. But now with shrill shout he poured forth his upbraidings upon goodly Agamemnon. . . . So spake Thersites, reviling Agamemnon, shepherd of the host, but goodly Odysseus came straight to his side, and looking sternly at him with hard words rebuked him: "Thersites, reckless in words, shrill orator though thou art, refrain thyself, nor aim to strive singly against kings. . . . But I will tell thee plain, and that I say shall even be brought to pass; if I find thee again raving as now thou art, then may Odysseus' head no longer abide upon his shoulders, . . . if I take thee not and strip from thee thy garments, thy mantle and tunic that cover thy nakedness, and for thyself send thee weeping to the fleet ships, and beat thee out of the assembly with shameful blows."

So spake he, and with his staff smote his back and shoulders: and he bowed down and a big tear fell from him, and a bloody weal stood up from his back beneath the golden sceptre.

Then he sat down and was amazed, and in pain with helpless look wiped away the tear. But the rest, though they were sorry, laughed lightly at him, and thus would one speak, looking at another standing by: "Go to, of a truth Odysseus hath wrought good deeds without number ere now . . but now is this thing the best by far. . . . Never again, forsooth, will his proud soul henceforth bid him revile the kings with slanderous words." So said the common sort. (Pages 28, 29.)

1. How many parts in the Homeric government? 2. What were they called? 3. Which part had the most power? 4. What would you call such a government? 5. How did the chief ruler evidently obtain office? 6. Did he have any insignia of office? 7. Was he distinguished outwardly from other men? (See I.—C.) 8. What officers assisted the ruler? 9. Did he live in an ostentatious manner? 10. Enumerate all his duties. 11. Who advised the chief ruler? 12. Was he obliged to accept this advice? 13. How did he make known his wishes to the people? 14. Were the people obliged to obey? 15. How could the ruler enforce his wishes? 16. Was he always successful? 17. By what right did he rule? 18. How was the second part of the government composed? 19. Who called it together? 20. What was done in it? 21. How was the session closed? 22. What was the use of such a body? 23. What was the third part of the government? 24. How was it composed? 25.

How was it called together? 26. Who presided over it? 27. Why was it called together? 28. Who had a right to speak in this gathering? 29. Should you say that the people enjoyed "freedom of speech"? 30. Were all on an equality? 31. What would you say of the treatment of Thersites? 32. What did the people think of it? 33. Describe an assembly, beginning with the summons. 34. Make an outline and write a narrative on the Government of the Homeric Age, citing the evidence for statements.

B. *Religion.*

Now when the twelfth morn thereafter was come, then the gods that are forever fared to Olympus all in company, led of Zeus. And Thetis forgat not her son's charge, but rose up from the sea wave, and at early morn mounted up to great heaven and Olympus. There found she Kronos's son of the far sounding voice sitting apart from all on the topmost peak of many-ridged Olympus. So she sat before his face and with her left hand clasped his knees, and with her right touched him beneath his chin, and spake in prayer to king Zeus, son of Kronos. . . . So spake she: but Zeus, the cloud-gatherer said no word to her, and sat long time in silence. But even as Thetis had clasped his knees, so held she by him clinging and questioned him yet a second time: "Promise me now this thing verily and bow thy head thereto; or else deny me, seeing there is naught for thee to fear; that I may know full well how I, among all gods, am least in honor."

Then Zeus, the cloud-gatherer sore troubled spake to her: "Verily it is a sorry matter, if thou wilt set me at variance with Hera, whene'er she provoketh me with taunting words. . . . But do thou now depart again, lest Hera mark aught; and I will take thought for these things to fulfill them. Come now, I will bow my head to thee that thou mayest be of good courage; for that of my part is the surest token amid the immortals; no word of mine is revocable nor false nor unfulfilled when the bowing of my head hath pledged it."

Kronion spake and nodded his dark brow, and the ambrosial locks waved from the king's immortal head; and he made great Olympus quake.

Thus the twain took counsel and parted; she leaped therewith into the deep sea from glittering Olympus and Zeus fared to his own palace. All the gods in company arose from their seats before their father's face; neither ventured any to await his coming but they stood up all before him. So he sat him there upon his throne; but Hera saw and was not ignorant how the daughter of the ancient of the sea, Thetis, the silver-footed, had devised counsel with him.

Anon with taunting words spake she to Zeus, the son of Kronos: "Now who among the gods, thou crafty of mind, hath devised counsel with thee? It is ever thy good pleasure to hold aloof from me and in secret meditation to give thy judgments, nor of thine own good will hast thou ever brought thyself to declare unto me the thing thou purposest." . .

To her made answer Zeus, the cloud-gatherer: "Lady, ever art thou imagining nor can I escape thee; yet shalt thou in no wise have power to fulfil but wilt be the further from my heart. *. . . Abide thou in silence and harken to my bidding, lest all the gods that are in Olympus keep not off from thee my visitation, when I put forth my hands unapproachable against thee."

He said and Hera the ox-eyed queen was afraid and sat in silence, curbing her heart; but throughout Zeus' palace the gods of heaven were troubled. (Pages 16–19.)

Now all other gods and chariot driving men slept all night long, only Zeus was not holden of sweet sleep; rather was he pondering in his mind how he should do honor to Achilles and destroy many beside the Achaians' ships.

And this design seemed to his mind the best, to-wit, to send a baneful dream upon Agamemnon, son of Atreus. So he spake and uttered to him winged words: "Come now, thou baneful Dream, go to the Achaians's fleet ships, enter into the hut of Agamemnon, son of Atreus, and tell him every word plainly as I charge thee. Bid him call to arms the flowing haired Achaians with all speed, for that now he may take the wide-wayed city of the Trojans. (Page 21.)

And they did sacrifice each man to one of the everlasting gods, praying for escape from death and the tumult of battle. But Agamemnon king of men slew a fat bull of five years to most mighty Kronion, and called the elders, the princes of the Achaian host. . . . Then stood they around the bull and took the barley meal, and Agamemnon made his prayer in their midst and said: "Zeus most glorious, most great god of the storm cloud, that dwellest in the heavens, vouchsafe that the sun set not upon us, nor the darkness come near until I have laid low upon the earth Priam's palace smurched with smoke and burnt the doorways thereof with consuming fire and rent on Hector's breast his doublet, cleft with the blade and about him may full many of his comrades, prone in the dust, bite the earth." . . .

Now when they had prayed and scattered the barley meal,

they first drew back the bull's head and cut his throat and flayed him and cut slices from the thighs and wrapped them in fat, making a double fold and laid raw collops thereon. And these they burnt on cleft wood stripped of leaves and spitted the vitals and held them over Hephaistos' flame. Now when the thighs were burnt and they had tasted the vitals then sliced they all the rest and pierced it through with spits and roasted it carefully and drew all off again. So when they had rest from the task and had made ready the banquet, they feasted nor was their heart aught stinted of the fair banquet. (Pages 33, 34.)

1. In what ways did the gods and goddesses resemble mortals? 2. In what ways were they unlike them? 3. Where did the gods live? 4. Did Thetis show much human nature in her treatment of Zeus? 5. Why did Zeus hesitate to grant her request? 6. Is his feeling very godlike? 7. Did Zeus apparently keep *all* his promises? 8. Did the gods love Zeus? 9. How did Hera know what Zeus had been doing? 10. Did her language show that she respected him? 11. Does their language indicate that their domestic life was happy? 12. Was the method taken by Zeus to quiet his wife a godlike one? 13. Why were the gods troubled? 14. How did the gods communicate with mortals? 15. How did mortals communicate with the gods? 16. Why did Agamemnon pray to Zeus? 17. Was his prayer a righteous one? 18. How did mortals try to win the favor of the gods? 19. Describe such a scene.

C. *Warfare.*

And the son of Atreus cried aloud and bad the Argives arm them and himself amid them did on the flashing bronze. First he fastened fair greaves about his legs, fitted with ankle clasps of silver, next, again, he did his breast-plate about his breast. . . . And round his shoulders he cast his sword wherein shone studs of gold, but the scabbard about it was silver fitted with golden chains. And he took the richly dight shield of his valor that covereth all the body of a man, a fair shield and round about it were ten circles of bronze and thereon were twenty white bosses of tin and one in the midst of black Cyanus . . . and on his head Agamemnon set a sturdy helm with a fourfold crest and a plume of horse hair, and terribly the crest nodded from above. And he grasped two strong spears shod with bronze and keen. . . .

Then each man gave in charge his horses to his charioteer to hold them in by the fosse, well and orderly, and themselves as heavy men at arms were hasting about being harnessed in their gear. . . . And long before the charioteers were they arrayed at the fosse but after them a little way came up the drivers. (Pages 202, 203.)

He spake and dashed Peisandros from his chariot to the earth, smiting him with his spear upon the breast and he lay supine upon the ground. But Hippolochos rushed away and him too he smote to earth and cut off his hands and his neck with the sword then tossed him like a ball of stone to roll through the throng. Then left he them, and where thickest clashed the battalions, there he set on and with him all the well-greaved Achaians. Footmen kept slaying footmen as they were driven in flight and horsemen slaying horsemen with the sword and from beneath them rose up the dust from the plain stirred by the thundering hoofs of horses. And the lord Agamemnon, ever slaying, followed after calling on the Argives. . . . So beneath Agamemnon, son of Atreus, fell the heads of the Trojans as they fled; and many strong necked horses rattled empty cars along the highways of the battle lacking their noble charioteers; but they on the earth were lying far more dear to the vultures than to their wives. (Pages 206, 207.)

Even so Lord Agamemnon, son of Atreus, followed hard on the Trojans ever slaying the hindmost man and they were scattered in flight and on face or back many of them fell from their chariots beneath the hand of Agamemnon, for mightily he raged with the spear. (Pages 207, 208.)

But Hector with his harness leaped from the chariot to the ground and shaking his sharp spears went through all the hosts stirring up his men to fight and he roused the dread din of battle.

And they wheeled round and stood and faced the Achaians while the Argives on the other side strengthened their battalions. And battle was made ready and they stood over against each other and Agamemnon first rushed in being eager to fight far in front of all. (Page 209.)

But Agamemnon son of Atreus of the wide domain smote Isos on the breast . . . with his spear, but Antiphos he struck hard by the ear with the sword and dashed him from the chariot. Then made he haste and stripped from them their goodly harness. (Page 205.)

So spake he and smote the fair maned horses with the shrill sounding whip and they felt the lash and fleetly bore the swift chariot among the Trojans and the Achaians turning on the dead and the shields and with blood besprinkled all the axle tree beneath and the rims round the car with the drops from the hoofs of the horses and with drops from the tires about the wheels. (Page 219.)

1. Describe the arms and armor of a Homeric king. 2. Did the kings fight like common soldiers? 3. Describe the uses of the different weapons and pieces of armor. 4. What advantage had a prince over a common man in battle? 5. Were the wounded and the dead kindly treated? 6. Point out some things that you consider barbarous. 7. Describe a Homeric battle. 8. Compare it with a modern battle.

II. MEANS OF UNIFICATION EXISTING AMONG THE GREEKS.

Pausanias: Description of Greece. 2 vols. George Bell & Sons, London, 1886. Strabo: Geography. 3 vols. George Bell & Sons, London, 1887. Herodotus: History of Persian Wars—Harper Bros., New York, 1891. Pindar: Odes of. Macmillan & Co., New York, 1892.

A. *Amphictyones.*

Some think that Amphictyon, the son of Deuca'ion, appointed the Great Council of the Greeks, and that was why those who assembled at the Council were called Amphictyones; but Androtion in his history of Attica says that originally delegates came to Delphi from the neighboring people who were called Amphictyones, and in process of time the name Amphictyones prevailed. . . . And in my time the Amphictyones were 30 members. Six came from Nicopolis, six from Macedonia, six from Thessaly, two from the Bœotians (who were originally in Thessaly and called Æolians), two from Phocis, and two from Delphi, one from Ancient Doris, one from the Locrians, called Ozolæ, one from the Locrians opposite Eubœa, one from Eubœa, one from Argos, Sicyon, Corinth and Megara, and one from Athens. Athens and Delphi and Nicopolis send delegates to every Amphictyonic Council: but the other cities I have mentioned only join the Amphictyonic Council at certain times. (Pausanias, vol. II, page 232.)

The Amphictyonic Council usually assembled at Oncestus, in the territory of Haliartus, near the lake Copaïs, and the Teneric Plain. It is situated on a height, devoid of trees, where is a temple of Neptune, also without trees. (Strabo, vol. II, page 109.)

As the situation of Delphi is convenient, persons easily

assembled there, particularly those from the neighborhood, of whom the Amphictyonic body is composed. It is the business of this body to deliberate on public affairs, and to it is more particularly entrusted the guardianship of the temple for the common good: for large sums of money were deposited there, and votive offerings, which required great vigilance and religious care. The early history of this body is unknown, but among the names which are recorded, Acrisius appears to have been the first to have regulated its constitution, to have determined what cities were to have votes in the council, and to have assigned the number of votes and mode of voting. To some cities he gave a single vote each, or a vote to two cities, or to several cities conjointly. He also defined the class of questions which might arise between the different cities, which were to be submitted to the decision of the Amphictyonic tribunals; and subsequently many other regulations were made, but this body, like that of the Achaians, was finally dissolved.

At first twelve cities are said to have assembled, each of which sent a Pylagoras. The convention was held twice a year, in spring and autumn. But latterly a greater number of cities assembled. They called both the vernal and the autumal convention Pylæan, because it was held at Pylæ, which has the name also of Thermopylæ. The Pylagoræ sacrificed to Ceres.

In the beginning, the persons in the neighborhood only assembled or consulted the oracle, but afterwards people repaired thither from a distance for this purpose, sent gifts, and constructed treasuries. . . . (Strabo, vol. II, page 118.)

1. What was an amphictyonic council? 2. How was it composed? 3. Which account of its foundation seems more probable to you? 4. Where did it meet? 5. How often? 6. What was its business? 7. Describe its organization. 8. Its method of transacting business.

B. *Oracles.*

We have remarked, that Parnassus itself is situated on the western boundaries of Phocis. The western side of this mountain is occupied by the Locri Ozolæ; on the southern is Delphi, a rocky spot, resembling in shape a theatre; on its summit is the oracle, and also the city which comprehends a circle of 16 stadia. Above it lies Lycoreia; here the Delphians were formerly settled above the temple. At present they live close to it around the Castalian Fountain. In front of the city, on the southern part, is Cirphis, a precipitous hill, leaving in the intermediate space a wooded ravine, through which the river Pleistus flows. Below Cirphis, near the sea, is Cirrha, from which there is an ascent to Delphi of about 80 stadia. (Strabo, vol. II, page 116.)

The temple at Delphi is now much neglected, although formerly it was held in the greatest veneration. Proofs of the respect which was paid to it are the treasuries constructed at the expense of communities and princes, where was deposited the wealth dedicated to sacred uses, the works of the most eminent artists, the Pythian games, and a multitude of celebrated oracles.

The place where the oracle is delivered is said to be a deep hollow cavern, the entrance to which is not very wide. From it rises an exhalation which inspires a divine frenzy: over the mouth is placed a lofty tripod on which the Pythian Princess ascends to receive the exhalation, after which she gives the prophet's response in verse or prose. The prose is adapted to measure by poets who are in the service of the temple. . . .

Although the highest honor was paid to this temple on account of the oracle, (for it was the most exempt of any from deception,) yet its reputation was owing in part to its situation in the center of all Greece, both within and without the isthmus. It was also supposed to be the center of the habitable earth. . . (Strabo, vol. II, pages 117, 118.)

And the temple which still exists was built by the Amphictyones out of the sacred money, and its architect was the Corinthian Spintharus. (Pausanius, vol. II, page 228.)

Gyges, having obtained the kingdom, sent many offerings to Delphi: for most of the silver offerings at Delphi are his; and besides the silver he gave a vast quantity of gold and among the rest, what is especially worthy mention, the bowls of gold, six in number, were dedicated by him. . . .
This Gyges is the first of the barbarians whom we know of that dedicated offerings at Delphi: except Midas, son of Gordius, king of Phrygia. For Midas dedicated the royal throne, on which he used to sit and administer justice, a piece of workmanship deserving of admiration. This throne stands in the same place as the bowls of Gyges. (Herodotus, pages 6, 7.)

After he (Crœsus) had formed this purpose, he determined to make trial as well of the oracles of Greece as that in Lydia; and sent different persons to different places, some to Delphi, some to Abæ of Phocis, and some to Dodona; others were sent Amphiaraus and Trophonius, and others to Branchidæ of Milesia.

These were the Grecian oracles to which Crœsus sent to consult. . . . But no soner had the Lydians entered the temple of Delphi to consult the god and ask the question enjoined them than the Pythian thus spoke in hexameter verse: "I know the number of the sands and the measure of the sea; I understand the dumb and hear him that does not speak; the savor of the hard-shell tortoise boiled in brass with the flesh of lamb strikes on my senses; brass is laid beneath it and brass is put over it."

The Lydians having written down this answer of the Pythian returned to Sardis. . . . When, however, he (Crœsus) heard that from Delphi, he immediately adored it, and approved of it, being convinced that the oracle at Delphi alone was a real oracle, because it had discovered what he had done. For when he had sent persons to consult the different oracles, watching the appointed day (Crœsus' instructions to his envoys were that computing the days from the time of their departure from Sardis, they should consult the oracle on the hundredth day by asking what Crœsus was then doing), he had recourse to the following contrivance: having thought what it was impossible to discover or guess at, he cut up a tortoise and a lamb, and boiled them himself together in a brazen caldron and put on it a cover of brass. (Herodotus, pages 18, 19.)

1. Make a diagram showing the location of the oracle and of the surrounding places as described by Strabo. (Look up Delphi on a map of Greece.) 2. Was the oracle respected throughout Grecian history? 3. Describe the manner in which an oracle was delivered. 4. From whom was the reply supposed to come? 5. Were the oracles always truthful? 6. Was Delphi really the "center of the habitable earth"? 7. What does this tell us about the geographical knowledge of the early Greeks? 8. What relation existed between the oracle and the Amphictyonic council? 9. Was the oracle famous? 10. Was its opinion valuable? 11. Were there other oracles besides Delphi? 12. Why did men consult the oracles? 13. Was it always an easy matter to understand the replies of the oracles? 14. Why were the replies given in such form?

C. *Games.*

From the time the Olympian games were revived continuously, prizes were first instituted for running, and Corœbus of Elis was the victor. His statue is at Olympia and his grave is on the borders of Elis. And in the 14th Olympiad afterwards the double course was introduced, when Hypenus, a native of Pisa, won the wild olive crown, and Acanthus the second. And in the 18th Olympiad they remembered the pentathlon and the wrestling. . . . And in the 23d Olympiad they ordained prizes for boxing. . . . And in the 25th Olympiad they had a race of full grown horses. . . . And in the 8th Olympiad late they introduced the pancratium and the riding race. The horse of Crannonian Crauxidas got in first, and the competitors for the pancratium were beaten by the Syracusan Lygdamus, who has his sepulcher at the stone quarries of Syracuse. And I don't know whether Lygdamus was really as big as the Theban Hercules, but that is the tradition at Syracuse. And the contest of the boys was not a revival of ancient usage, but the people of Elis instituted it because the idea pleased them. So prizes were instituted for running and wrestling among boys in the 307th Olympiad. . . . And in the 41st Olympiad afterwards they invited boxing boys. . . . And the race in heavy armor was tried in the 65th Olympiad as an exercise for war, I think; and of those who ran with their shields Damaretus of Heræum was the victor. . . .

The order of the games in our day is to sacrifice victims to the god and then to contend in the pentathlon and horse race, according to the programme established in the 77th Olympiad, for before this horses and men contended on the same day. And at that period the Pancratiasts did not appear till night for they could not compete sooner, so much time being taken up by the horse races and pentathlon. . . But in the 25th Olympiad afterwards nine general umpires were appointed, three for the horses, three to watch the pentathlon and three to preside over the remaining games. And in the 2d Olympiad after this a tenth umpire was appointed. And in the 103d Olympiad, as the people of Elis had twelve tribes, a general umpire was appointed by each. (Pausanias, vol. I, pages 316–318.)

(The following extracts are taken from the Odes of Pindar. They were written and sung in honor of the victors in the four great games, the Olympian, the Pythian, the Nemean and the Isthmian.)

O kindly Peace, daughter of Righteousness, thou that makest cities great and holdest the supreme keys of councils and of wars, welcome thou this honor to Aristomenes, won in the Pythian games. . . . So let that which lyeth in my path, my debt to thee, O boy, the youngest of thy country's glories, run on apace winged by my art.

For in wrestlings thou art following the footsteps of thy uncles, and shamest neither Theognetos at Olympia nor the victory that at Isthmos was won by Kleitomachos' stalwart limbs. (Pindar, page 89.)

I have·desire to proclaim with aid of the deep vested graces a victory at Pytho of Telesikrates bearing the shield of bronze, and to speak aloud his name, for his fair fortune and the glory wherewith he hath crowned Cyrene city of charioteers. (Pindar, page 92.)

Acharnai of old was famous for its men, and as touching games, the Timodenidai rank there pre-eminent. Beneath Parnassos' lordly height they won four victories in the games; moreover in the valleys of noble Pelops they have obtained eight crowns at the hands of the men of Corinth and seven at Nemea; and at home more than may be numbered at the games of Zeus:

To whose glory, O citizens, sing for Timodemos a song of triumph, and bring him in honor home, and chant our prelude tunefully. (Pindar, page 111.)

1. Describe the Olympic games as though you were a spectator, using the evidence given. 2. Did they have a religious character? 3. What prizes were granted to the victor? 4. Was it a great honor to be a victor at Olympus?

THE ATHENIAN CONSTITUTION.

CHAPTER II.

THE ATHENIAN CONSTITUTION.

Aristotle on the Athenian Constitution. Translated, with introduction and notes by F. G. Kenyon, M. A. London, George Bell & Sons. 1891.

The Athenian constitution, either written by Aristotle or under his direction, is one of our most valuable sources on this subject. An incomplete copy was discovered a few years ago in Egypt. Up to that time the work was known only by extracts found in other Greek writers. This discovery is one of the events of our century. Aristotle lived in the fourth century before Christ.

I. ENROLLMENT OF CITIZENS AND TRAINING OF YOUTHS.

The present (about 330 B. C.) state of the constitution is as follows: The franchise is open to all who are of citizen birth by both parents. They are enrolled among the demesmen* at the age of eighteen. On the occasion of their enrollment, the demesmen give their votes on oath, first as to whether they appear to be of the age prescribed by law (if not they are dismissed back into the ranks of the boys), and secondly as to whether the candidate is freeborn and of such parentage as the laws require. Then if they decide that he is not a free man, he appeals to the law courts and the demesmen appoint five of their own number to act as their accusers; and if the court decides that he has no right to be enrolled, he is sold by the state as a slave, but if he wins his case, he has a right to be enrolled among the demesmen without further question. After this the council examines

---
*The smallest subdivision of Attica was called a deme and the residents demesmen.

(18)

those who have been enrolled, and if it comes to the conclusion that any of them is less than eighteen years of age, it fines the demesmen who enrolled him. When the youths have passed this examination, their fathers meet by their tribes,* and appoint on oath three of their fellow-tribesmen, over forty years of age, who in their opinion are the best and most suitable persons to have charge of the youths; and of these the assembly elects one from each tribe as guardian, together with the superintendent chosen from the general body of Athenians, to control the whole. These persons take charge of the youths, and first of all they make the circuit of the temples; then they proceed to Piræs, and some of them garrison Munychia and some the south shore. The Assembly also elects two trainers, with subordinate instructors, who teach them to fight in heavy armour, to use the bow and javelin, and to discharge a catapult. The guardians receive from the state a drachma† apiece for their keep and the youths four obols‡ apiece. Each guardian receives the allowance for all the members of his tribe and buys the necessary provisions for the common stock (since they mess together by tribes), and generally superintends everything. In this way they spend the first year. The next year, when the assembly is held in the theater,§ after giving a public display of their military evolutions, they receive a shield and a spear from the state; after which they patrol the country and spend their time in the forts. For these two years they are on garrison duty and wear the military cloak, and during this time they are exempt from all taxes. They also can neither bring an action at law nor have one brought against them, in order that they may not be mixed up in civil business; though exception is made concerning actions concerning inheritances and wards of state, or of any sacrificial ceremony connected with the clan of any individual. When the two years have elapsed they at once take their position among the other citizens. Such is the manner of the enrollment of the citizens and of the training of the youth.

1. Under what conditions could a man become a citizen or Athens? 2. Compare those conditions with the conditions in our own country. 3. How many bodies might be

---

* The people were divided into ten tribes.
† Six obols.
‡ An obol was about three cents.
§ On the occasion of the great Dionysiac festival.

called upon to examine a man's claims to citizenship? 4. Why so many? 5. What class of men was without political rights? 6. Explain the course followed in the selection of guardians, *i. e.*, why does the assembly of all the citizens select at once all the guardians? 7. Why was the "circuit of the temples" made? 8. Why were the youths obliged to give two years to military duty? 9. Why did the state support them and free them from taxes and lawsuits? 10. What was the reason for the presentation of the shield and spear?

II. THE PRYTANES.

All the magistrates that are concerned with the ordinary routine of administration are elected by lot, except the Military Treasurer, the Commissioners of the Theoric fund * and the Superintendent of Springs.† These are elected by vote, and the magistrates thus elected hold office from one Panathenaic festival to another. All military officers are also elected by vote. The council of five hundred is elected by lot, fifty from each tribe. Each tribe holds the office of Prytanes‡ in turn, the order being determined by lot; the first four serve for thirty-six days each, the last six for thirty-five, since the reckoning is by lunar years. The Prytanes for the time being, in the first place, mess together in the Tholus, and receive a sum of money from the state for their maintenance; and secondly they convene the meetings of the Council and the Assembly. The Council they convene every day unless it is a holiday, the Assembly four times in each prytany. It is also their duty to draw up the programme of the matters with which the Council has to deal, and to decide what subjects are to be dealt with on each particular day, and what are not within its competence. They also draw up the programme for the meetings of the Assembly (pp. 77-82).

1. Why were all of the officers not elected by lot? 2. How long was the term of office? 3. By whom was the work of the council and assembly controlled? 4. How often did this controlling body change? 5. What would be the objection to such an organization in a large state?

III. THE COUNCIL.

The Council passes judgment on nearly all magistrates, especially those who have the control of money; its judg-

---

* Fund that provided the populace with the price of admission to the theatre.

† Athens was scantily supplied with fresh water.

‡ Presidents of the Council and Assembly in the fifth century. Later the Prytanes appointed the presidents.

ment, however, is not final, but is subject to an appeal to the law-courts. Private individuals, also, may impeach any magistrate they please for not obeying the laws, but here too there is an appeal to the law-courts, if the Council declare the charge proved. The Council also examines those who are to be its members for the ensuing year, and also the nine Archons. Formerly the Council had full power to reject candidates for office as unsuitable, but now these too have an appeal to the law-courts. In all these matters, therefore, the Council has no final jurisdiction. It has, however, a preliminary jurisdiction of all matters brought before the Assembly, and the Assembly cannot vote on any question unless it has first been considered by the Council and placed on the programme by the Prytanes; since a person who carries a motion in the Assembly is liable to an action for illegal proposal on these grounds (p. 85.)

1. In what way did the state protect itself against corrupt officials? 2. What resort had the official who was unjustly attacked? 3. In all cases of this kind, and in all cases between the government and the citizen, what seems to have been the final resort? 4. Had it always been so? 5. What was the relation of the Council to the Assembly? 6. How would a citizen be treated who induced the assembly to agree to anything not proposed by the Prytanes?

IV. THE TREASURERS AND COMMISSIONERS.

The Council also co-operates with the other magistrates in most of their duties. First, there are the treasurers of Athena, ten in number, elected by lot, one from each tribe. According to the law of Solon—which is still in force—they must be Pentacosiomedimni,† but in point of fact the person on whom the lot falls holds the office even though he be quite a poor man. These officers take over charge of the Statue of Athena, the figures of Victory and all other ornaments of the temple, together with the money, in the presence of the Council. Then there are the commissioners for public contracts, ten in number, one elected by lot from each tribe. These officers farm out the public contracts and lease the mines, and in conjunction with the military treasurer and the Commissioners of the Theoric fund, confirm the farming out of taxes in the presence of the Council, to the persons whom the latter appoints. They also lease, in the presence of the Council, such workable mines as are let out by the state, which are let for three years, and the conces-

---

† The citizens of Athena were divided into classes on the basis of incomes. The Pentacosiomedimni had an income of five hundred measures, liquid or solid.

sions which are let for (three) years, and also the property of those who have gone into exile from a sentence of the Areopagus, and of state debtors; and the nine Archons ratify the contracts. They also hand over to the Council lists of the taxes which are farmed out for the year, entering on whitened tablets the name of the lessee and the amount paid (pp. 86-88).

1. Was the Athens of Aristotle's time more democratic than the Athens of Solon's day? 2. What sources of income did the state have? 3. Which of these sources is looked upon as unjust to-day? 4. Why did the officers always make the contracts in the presence of the Council? 5. Do we farm out our taxes?

V. Receivers-General, Auditors, and Examiners.

There are ten Receivers-General, elected by lot, one from each tribe. These officers receive the tablets, and strike off the instalments as they are paid, in the presence of the Council in the Council-chamber, and give the tablets back to the public clerk. If any one fails to pay his instalment, a note is made of it from this record, together with the cause; and he is bound to make good the deficiency, or, in default, to be imprisoned. The Council has full power by the laws to exact this payment and to inflict this imprisonment. They receive the money, therefore, on one day and portion it out among the magistrates; and on the next day they bring up the report of the apportionment, written on a wooden notice-board, and read it out in the Council-chamber, after which they ask publicly in the Council whether any one knows of any malpractice in reference to the apportionment, on the part of either a magistrate or a private individual, and if any one is charged with malpractice they put the question to the vote.

The Council also elects ten Auditors by lot from its own members, to audit the accounts of the magistrates for each prytany. They also elect one Examiner of Accounts by lot from each tribe with two assessors for each examiner, whose duty it is to sit in the market place, each opposite the statue of the eponymous hero of his tribe; and if any one wishes, on the ground of some private difference, to question the accounts of any magistrate who has given in his account before the law-courts, within three days of his having given them in, the assessor enters on a whitened tablet the name of the person and that of the magistrate prosecuted, together with the malpractice that is alleged against him. Then he enters his claim for a penalty of such amount as seems to him fitting, and gives in the record to the examiner. The latter takes it and hears the charge and if he considers it proved, he hands it over, if a private case, to the local justices who introduce cases for the tribe concerned, while if a public case he enters it on the register of the Thesmothetæ.* Then if the Thesmothetæ accept it, they bring the accounts of this magistrate once more before the law-court and the decision of the jury stands as the final judgment (pp. 89–90).

1. Are citizens imprisoned to-day for non-payment of taxes? 2. What two great safeguards against fraud do we see employed throughout the Athenian government? 3. Show how they would be effective.

VI. OTHER COMMISSIONERS.

The Council also examines infirm paupers; for there is a law which enacts that a person possessing less than three minas, who are so crippled as not to be able to do any work, are, after examination by the Council, to receive two obols a day from the state for their support. A treasurer is appointed by lot to attend to them.

The Council also, speaking broadly, co-operates in most of the duties of all of the other magistrates; and this ends the list of the functions of that body. There are ten Commissioners for Repairs of Temples, elected by lot, who receive the sum of thirty minas from the Receivers-General, and therewith carry out the most necessary repairs in the temples.

There are also ten City Commissioners, of whom five hold office in Piræus and five in the city. Their duty is to see that female flute and harp and lute players are not hired at more than two drachmas, and if more than one person is anxious to hire the same girl, they cast lots and hire her to the person to whom the lot falls. They also provide that no collector of sewage shall shoot any of his sewage within ten stadia of the walls; they prevent people from blocking up the streets by building or stretching barriers across them, or making drain pipes in mid-air so as to pour their contents into the streets, or having doors which open outwards; and they remove the corpses of those who die in the street, for which purpose they have a body of state slaves assigned to them.

Market Commissioners are elected by lot, five for Piræus,

---

*Six in number, were the junior Archons.

five for the city. The duty assigned to them by law is to see that all articles offered for sale in the market are pure and unadulterated.

Commissioners of Weights and Measures are elected by lot, five for the city and five for Piræus. They see that sellers use fair weights and measures.

Formerly there were five Corn Commissioners, elected by lot for Piræus, and five for the city; but now there are twenty for the city and fifteen for Piræus. Their duties are, first, to see that the unprepared corn in the market is offered for sale at reasonable prices, and secondly, to see that the millers sell barley meal at a price proportionate to that of barley; and that the bakers sell their loaves at a price proportionate to that of wheat, and of such weight as the Commissioners may appoint; for the law requires them to fix the standard weight.

There are ten Superintendents of the Mart, elected by lot, whose duty it is to superintend the Mart, and to compel merchants to bring up into the city two-thirds of the corn which is brought by sea to the Corn Mart.

The Eleven are also appointed by lot to take care of those who are in the state gaol. Thieves, kidnappers, and pickpockets are brought to them, and if they plead guilty, they are executed, but if they deny their crime the Eleven bring the case before the law-courts; if the prisoners are acquitted they release them, but if not, they execute them. They also bring up before the law-courts the list of farms and houses claimed as state property; and if it is decided that they are so, they deliver them to the Commissioners for Public Contracts. The Eleven also bring up informations laid against magistrates alleged to be disqualified; this function comes within their province, but some such cases are brought up by the Thesmothetæ. (pp. 92-95.)

1. How did the Athenians take care of their paupers? 2. Did the Athenians have a state religion? 3. Point out all the curious things that you note in the work of the commissioners and tell why they are curious. 4. How many o these things are regulated by our government? 5. How many do we consider it unwise to regulate, and why? 6. Was the treatment of thieves, kidnappers, and pickpockets wise?

VII. COMMISSIONERS (CONT.).

The following magistrates also are elected by lot: Ten Commissioners of Roads, who, with an assigned body of public slaves, are required to keep the roads in order; and ten Auditors, with ten assistants, to whom all persons who have held any office must give in their accounts. These are the only officers who audit the accounts of those who are subject to examination, and who bring them up for examination before the law-courts. If they detect any magistrate in embezzlement, the jury condemn him on the charge of embezzlement, and he is obliged to repay ten-fold the sum he is declared to have misappropriated. If they charge a magistrate with accepting bribes and the jury convict him, they fine him for corruption, and this sum too is repaid ten-fold. Or if they convict him of unfair dealing, he is fined on that charge, and the sum assessed is paid without increase, if payment is made before the ninth prytany, but otherwise it is doubled. A ten-fold fine is not doubled, however.

The Clerk of the Pyrtany, as he is called, is also elected by lot. He is the chief of all the clerks and keeps the resolutions which are passed by the Assembly, and records of all other business, and attends at the sessions of the Council. Formerly, he was elected by open vote and the most distinguished and trustworthy persons were elected to the post, as is known from the fact that the name of this officer is appended on the pillars recording treaties of alliance and grants of consulship and citizenship. Now, however, he is elected by lot. There is, in addition, a Clerk of Laws, elected by lot, who attends at the sessions of the Council, and he too records all the laws. The Assembly also elects by open vote a clerk to read documents to it and to the Council; he has not other duty except that of reading aloud.

The Assembly also elects, by lot, ten Commissioners of Religion, known as the Commissioners for Sacrifices, who offer the sacrifices appointed by oracle, and, in conjunction with the seers, take the auspices whenever there is occasion (pp. 98-100).

1. What difference between road repairing in Attica and in our country? 2. Was the Athenian method of auditing accounts similar to our own? 3. Does our method of punishment in case of embezzlement differ from theirs? 4. What modern state officers resemble the Clerk of the Prytany, the Clerk of Laws, and the Clerk of the Assembly?

VIII. THE ARCHONS.

All the foregoing magistrates are elected by lot, and their duties are those which have been stated. To pass on to the nine Archons, as they are called, the manner of their ap-

pointment from the earliest times has been described already
At the present day, six Thesmothetæ are elected by lot, together with their clerk, and in addition to these an Archon, a King, and a Polemarch. One is elected from each tribe. They are examined first of all by the Council of Five Hundred, with the exception of the clerk. The latter is examined only in the law-court, like other magistrates (for all magistrates, whether elected by lot or open vote, are examined before entering on their offices); but the nine Archons are examined both in the Council and again in the law-court. Formerly, no one could hold the office if the Council rejected him, but now there is an appeal to the law-court which is the final authority in the matter of the examination. When they are examined, they are asked first, "Who is your father, and of what deme? who is your father's father? who is your mother? who is your mother's father, and of what deme?" Then the candidate is asked whether he possesses an ancestral Apollo and a household Zeus, and where their sanctuaries are; next if he possesses a family tomb, and where; then if he treats his parents well, and pays his taxes and has served on the required military expeditions. When the examiner has put these questions, he proceeds, "Call the witnesses to these facts;" and when the candidate has produced his witnesses he next asks, "Does any one wish to make any accusation against this man?" If an accuser appears he gives the parties an opportunity of making their accusation and defence, and then puts it to the Council to pass the candidate or not, and to the law-court to give the final vote. If no one wishes to make an accusation, he proceeds at once to the vote. Formerly a single individual gave the vote, but now all the members are obliged to vote on the candidates, so if any unprincipled candidate has managed to get rid of his accusers, it may still be possible for him to be disqualified before the law-court. When the examination has been thus completed, they proceed to the stone on which are the pieces of the victims, and on which the arbitrators take oath before declaring their decisions, and witnesses swear to their testimony. On this stone the Archons stand and swear to execute their office uprightly and according to the laws, and not to receive presents in respect of the performance of the duties or, if they do, to dedicate a golden statue. When they have taken this oath, they proceed to the Acropolis, and there they repeat it; after this they enter upon their office.

The Archon, the King, and the Polemarch have each two assessors; they appoint whomsoever they please to the post, but the nominees are examined in the law-court before they begin to act, and give in accounts on each occasion of their acting.

As soon as the Archon enters office, he begins by issuing a proclamation that whatever any one possessed before he entered the office, that he shall possess and hold until the end of his term (pp. 101–103).

1. What was the object of each of the questions asked of the newly elected officers? 2. What do the changes in the form of the procedure tell you of the development of the constitution? 3. Why did the Archons take oath standing on the stone? 4. What is the meaning of the proclamation of the Archon?

IX. Commissioners of Games.

There are also ten Commissioners of Games, elected by lot, one from each tribe. These officers, after passing an examination, serve for four years; and they manage the Panathenaic procession, the contest in music and that in gymnastic, and the horse-race; they also, in conjunction with the Council, see to the making of the robe of Athena, and the vases, and they present the oil to the athletes. This oil is collected from the sacred olives. The Archon requisitions it from the owners of the farms on which the sacred olives grow, to the amount of three-quarters of a pint from each plant. Formerly, the state used to sell the fruit itself, and if anyone dug up or broke down one of the sacred olives, he was tried by the Council of Areopagus, and if he was condemned, the penalty was death. Since, however, the oil has been paid by the owner of the farm, the procedure has lapsed, though the law remains. The State takes the oil from the shoots, not from the stem of the plants. When then the Archon has collected his oil for his year of office, he hands it over to the Treasurers, to preserve in the Acropolis until the Panathenæa, when they measure it out to the Commissioners of Games, and they again to the victorious competitors. The prizes for the victors in the musical contest consist of silver and gold, for the victors in manly vigor, of shields, and for the victors in the gymnastic contest and the horse-race, of oil.

All officers connected with military service are elected by open vote. The generals were formerly elected one from each tribe, but now they are chosen from the whole mass of citizens (pp. 110–112).

1. Why were the games so important? (See the extracts in the September MONTHLY). 2. Why was it such a crime to injure the olives? 3. Why should the oil be given to victors in gymnastic contests and horse-races? 4. Which was the better, the earlier or later way of electing a general?

X. ELECTION AND PAY OF MAGISTRATES.

Of the magistrates elected by lot in former times some, including the nine Archons, were elected out of the tribe as a whole, while others, namely those who are now elected in the Theseum, were appointed among the demes; but since the demes used to sell the elections, these magistrates too are now elected from the whole tribe, except the members of the council and the guards of the dock-yards, who are still left to the demes.

Pay is received for the following services: First, the members of the Assembly receive a drachma for the ordinary meetings, and nine obols for the "sovereign" meeting. Then the jurors at the law-courts receive three obols; and the members of the council, five obols. The Prytanes receive an allowance for their maintenance. . . . The nine Archons receive four obols apiece for maintenance, and also keep a herald and a flute player; and the Archon for Salamis receives a drachma a day. The Commissioners for Games dine in the Prytaneum during the month of Hecatombæon in which the Panthenaic festival takes place, from the fourteenth day onwards. The Amphictyonic deputies to Delos receive a drachma a day from the exchequer of Delos. Also all magistrates sent to Samos, Scyros, Lemnos, or Imbros receive an allowance for their maintenance.

The military offices may be held any number of times, but none of the others more than once, except the membership of the Council, which may be held twice (pp. 114-115).

1. Was the new method of electing magistrates better than the old? 2. Why should a citizen be allowed to hold military offices any number of times, but not the others? 3. Were the officers well paid?

XI. THE JURIES.

The juries for the law-courts are chosen by lot by the nine Archons, each for their own tribe, and by the clerk to the Thesmothetæ for the tenth. There are ten entrances into the court, one for each tribe; a hundred chests, ten for each tribe; and ten other chests in which are placed the tickets of the jurors on whom the lot falls. Also two vases and a number of staves, equal to that of the jurors required, are placed by the side of each entrance; and counters are put into one vase equal in number to the staves. These are inscribed with letters of the alphabet beginning with eleventh (lambda), equal in number to the courts which require to be filled. All persons above thirty years of age are qualified to serve as jurors, provided they are not debtors to the state and have not lost their civil rights. If any unqualified person serves as juror, an information is laid against him, and he is brought before the court; and, if he is convicted, the jurors assess the punishment or fine which they consider him to deserve. If he is condemned to a money fine, he must be imprisoned till he has paid up both the original debt, on account of which the information was laid against him, and also the fine which the court has laid upon him. Each juror has a ticket of box-wood on which is inscribed his name with the name of his father and his deme, and one of the letters of the alphabet up to kappa; for the jurors are divided into ten sections according to their tribes, with approximately an equal number from each tribe in each letter. When the Thesmothetes has decided by lot which letters are required to attend at the courts, the servant puts up above each court the letter which has been assigned to it by the lot (pp. 115–116).

1. Do the law-courts play an important part in the life of Athens? Give all the proofs that can be found in the above extracts. 2. Were they more influential in Aristotle's day than before? 3. What subdivision of the Athenian people runs through the whole constitution? 4. Cite all the cases of it found in the extracts. 5. In what things do the Athenians appear to be undemocratic and illiberal judged by our standards?

SPARTAN LIFE.

CHAPTER III.

SPARTAN LIFE.

Xenophon: The Hellenica. Translated by H. G. Dakyns, M. A. 2 vols. Macmillan & Co., New York, 1892.

CONTRARY to the usual practice, I have chosen the material for the study of "Spartan Life" from the writings of Xenophon, instead of from the "Life of Lycurgus" by Plutarch. I did this for two reasons: the first was a matter of expediency and the second of method. Plutarch's lives are in the hands of every boy and girl. The works of Xenophon are not. Moreover, Xenophon's "Polity of the Lacedæmonians," contained in the second volume with the "Hellenica," is probably one of the oldest of Plutarch's sources. For in the introduction to his "Life of Lycurgus" he mentions as his sources Xenophon (444 B. C.), Aristotle (384 B. C.), Timæus (359 B. C.), Eratosthenes (272 B. C.), Apollodorus (150 B. C.). Plutarch himself was born about 50 A. D. All these dates are, of course, only approximate. Xenophon, it would seem, lived some five hundred years before Plutarch, and consequently five hundred years nearer the time of Lycurgus—if Lycurgus ever lived at all.

Plutarch, in writing of the beginnings of Spartan government, bore the same time relation to his subject that I should bear to my subject were I to write the history of the First Crusade (1096). And if, in writing this history, I made use of the works of a writer who in 1396 wrote about the First Crusade, that writer would stand between me and my subject just as Xenophon stands between Plutarch and his subject.

In making use of these extracts from Xenophon one thing should not be forgotten. When he speaks of Spartan institutions as they existed in his day he speaks as an eye witness and as a competent one, too. He was an intimate friend of the Spartan king, Agesilaus, lived for a long time in the vicinity of Sparta, and as a general of ability was a competent judge of the Spartan military system. An excellent exercise would be a comparison of these extracts with the portions of Plutarch that deal with the same topics.

SPARTAN SUPREMACY AND SPARTAN INSTITUTIONS.

I recall the astonishment with which I first noted the unique position of Sparta amongst the states of Hellas, the relatively sparse population, and at the same time the extraordinary powers and prestige of the community. I was puzzled to account for the fact. It was only when I came to consider the peculiar institutions of the Spartans, that my wonderment ceased. Or rather, it is transferred to the legislator who gave them those laws, obedience to which has been the secret of their prosperity.' This legislator, Lycurgus, I must needs admire, and hold him to have been one of the wisest of mankind. Certainly he was no servile imitator of other states. It was by a stroke of invention rather, and on a pattern much in opposition to the commonly accepted one, that he brought his fatherland to this pinacle of prosperity. (Vol. II, 295.)

QUESTIONS.

1. What object did Xenophon evidently have in writing his "Polity of the Lacedæmonians"? 2. Why should the fact stated in the first sentence puzzle him? 3. How did he finally explain it? 4. Did it necessarily follow that Lycurgus had lived, because Xenophon saw in Sparta certain institutions attributed to Lycurgus?

EDUCATION OF CHILDREN.

I wish now to explain the systems of education in fashion here and elsewhere. Throughout the rest of

Hellas the custom on the part of those who claimed to educate their sons in the best way is as follows: As soon as the children are of an age to understand what is said to them they are immediately placed under the charge of Paidagogoi (or Tutors), who are also attendants, and sent off to the school of some teacher to be taught "grammar," "music," and the concerns of the Palestra*. Besides this they are given shoes to wear which tend to make their feet tender, and their bodies are enervated by various changes of clothing. And as for food, the only measure recognized is that which is fixed by appetite.

But when we turn to Lycurgus, instead of leaving it to each member of the state privately to appoint a slave to be his son's tutor, he set over the young Spartans a public guardian, the Paidonomos or "Pastor," to give him his proper title, with complete authority over them. This guardian was selected from those who filled the highest magistracies. He had authority to hold musters of the boys, and as their overseer, in case of any misbehavior, to chastise severely. The legislator further provided the pastor with a body of youths in the prime of life and bearing whips to inflict punishment when necessary, with this happy result, that in Sparta modesty and obedience ever go hand in hand, nor is there lack of either.

Instead of softening their feet with shoe or sandal, his rule was to make them hardy through going barefoot. This habit, if practiced, would, as he believed, enable them to scale heights more easily and clamber down precipices with less danger. In fact, with his feet so trained the young Spartan would leap and spring and run faster unshod than another shod in the ordinary way.

Instead of making them effeminate with a variety of clothes, his rule was to habituate them to a single garment the whole year through, thinking that so they would be better prepared to withstand the variations of heat and cold.

Again, as regards food, according to his regulation, the Eiren, or head of the flock, must see that his messmates gather to the club meal with such moderate food as to avoid that heaviness which is engendered by repletion and yet not to remain altogether unacquainted

---
* Wrestling school.

with the pains of penurious living. His belief was that by such training in boyhood they would be better able when occasion demanded to continue toiling on an empty stomach. They would be all the fitter, if the word of command were given, to remain on the stretch for a long time without extra dieting. The craving for luxuries would be less, the readiness to take any victuals set before them greater, and, in general, the regime would be found more healthy. Under it he thought the lads would increase in stature and shape into finer men, since, as he maintained, a dietary which gave suppleness to the limbs must be more conducive to both ends than one which added thickness to the bodily parts by feeding.

On the other hand, to guard against a too great pinch of starvation, though he did not actually allow the boys to help themselves without further trouble to what they needed more, he did give them permission to steal this thing or that in the effort to alleviate their hunger. It was not of course from any real difficulty how else to supply them with nutriment that he left it with them to provide themselves by this crafty method. Nor can I conceive that any one will so misinterpret the custom. Clearly its explanation lies in the fact, that he who would live the life of a robber must forego sleep by night, and in the daytime he must employ shifts and lie in ambuscade; he must prepare and make ready his scouts, etc., if he is to succeed in capturing the quarry. (Vol. II, 297-301.)

QUESTIONS.

1. What object did the Spartans evidently have in view in educating their children? Give full proof. 2. Did the training accomplish this end? (See Public Mess-rooms). 3. What would you criticise in the system? 4. How would the Spartan reply to your criticisms? 5. Name all that was really good in the system?

TRAINING OF THE YOUTH.

Coming to the critical period at which a boy ceases to be a boy and becomes a youth, we find that it is just then that the rest of the world proceeds to emancipate their children from the private tutor and the schoolmaster, and, without substituting any further ruler, are content to launch them into absolute independence.

Here, again, Lycurgus took an entirely opposite view

of the matter. This, if observation might be trusted, was the season when the tide of animal spirit flows fast and a froth of insolence rises to the surface; when, too, the most violent appetites for divers pleasures, in serried ranks invade the mind. This, then, was the right moment, at which to impose ten fold labors upon the growing youth, and to devise for him a subtle system of absorbing occupation. And by a crowning enactment, which said that "He who shrank from the duties imposed on him, would forfeit henceforth all claim to the glorious honors of the state," he caused, not only the public authorities, but those personally interested in the several companies of youths to take serious pains so that no single individual of them should by an act of craven cowardice find himself utterly rejected and reprobate within the body politic.

Furthermore, in his desire firmly to implant in their youthful souls a root of modesty, he imposed upon these bigger boys a special rule. In the very streets they were to keep their two hands within the folds of their coat; they were to walk in silence and without turning their heads to gaze, now here, now there, but rather to keep their eyes fixed upon the ground before them. And hereby it would seem to be proved conclusively that, even in the matter of quiet bearing and sobriety, the masculine type may claim greater strength than that which we attribute to the nature of women. At any rate, you might sooner expect a stone image to find voice than one of those Spartan youths; to divert the eyes of some bronze statue were less difficult. And as to quiet bearing, no bride ever stepped in bridal bower with more natural modesty. Note them when they have reached the public table. The plainest answer to the question asked,—that is all you need expect to hear from their lips. (Vol. II, 302-303.)

QUESTIONS.

1. Which of the two methods of dealing with youth—described by Xenophon—was the more scientific? Why? 2. What three things did the Spartans insist upon? 3. What were the good results produced by this training? 4. What kind of weakness did the Spartan especially abhor?

PUBLIC MESS-ROOMS.

The above is a fairly exhaustive statement of the institutions tracable to the legislature of Lycurgus in connection with the successive stages of a citizen's life. It remains that I should endeavor to describe the style of living which he established for the whole body, irrespective of age. It will be understood that, when Lycurgus first came to deal with the question, the Spartans, like the rest of the Hellenes, used to mess privately at home. Tracing more than half the current misdemeanors to this custom, he was determined to drag his people out of holes and corners into the broad daylight, and so he invented the public mess-rooms. Whereby he expected at any rate to minimize the transgression of orders.

As to food, his ordinance allowed them so much as, while not inducing repletion, should guard them from actual want. And, in fact, there are many exceptional dishes in the shape of game supplied from the hunting field. Or, as a substitute for these, rich men will occasionally garnish the feast with wheaten loaves. So that from beginning to end, till the mess breaks up the common board is never stinted for viands nor yet extravagantly furnished.

So also in the matter of drink. While putting a stop to all unnecessary potations, detrimental alike to a firm brain and a steady gait, he left them free to quench thirst when nature dictated; a method which would at once add to the pleasure whilst it diminished the danger of drinking. And indeed one may fairly ask how, on such a system of common meals, it would be possible for any one to ruin either himself or his family through either gluttony or wine bibbing.

This, too, must be borne in mind, that in other states equals in age, for the most part, associate together, and such an atmosphere is little conducive to modesty. Whereas in Sparta, Lycurgus was careful so to blend the ages that the younger men must benefit largely by the experience of the elders. . . . Amongst other good results obtained through this outdoor system of meals may be mentioned these: There is the necessity of walking home when a meal is over, and a consequent anxiety not to be caught tripping under the influence of wine, since they all know of course that the supper table must be presently abandoned and that they must move as freely in the dark as in the day, even the help of a torch to guide the steps being forbidden to all on active service.

At any rate, it would be hard to discover a healthier or more completely developed human being, physically speaking, than the Spartan. Their gymnastic training, in fact, makes demands alike on the legs and arms and neck, et cetera, simultaneously. (Vol. II, 305-307.)

QUESTIONS.

1. Is there any relation between the eating and drinking of the Spartan and his ideal? 2. What was his ideal? Prove it. 3. Did the Spartan condemn hard drinking because it was immoral? 4. What prevented the adult Spartan from violating the rules? 5. Point out all the good effects of these common meals.

AN ILL-STARRED EXISTENCE FOR THE COWARD.

The following, too, may well excite our admiration for Lycurgus. I speak of the consummate skill with which he induced the whole state of Sparta to regard an honorable death as preferable to an ignoble life. And indeed, if any one will investigate the matter, he will find that by comparison with those who make it a principle to retreat in face of danger, actually fewer of these Spartans die in battle since, to speak truth, salvation, it would seem, attends on virtue far more frequently than on cowardice. . . .

Yet the actual means by which he gave currency to these principles is a point which it were well not to overlook. It is clear that the lawgiver set himself deliberately to provide all the blessings of heaven for the good man, and a sorry and ill-starred existence for the coward.

In other states the man who shows himself base and cowardly, wins to himself an evil reputation and the nickname of a coward, but that is all. For the rest he buys and sells in the same market place with a good man; he sits beside him at the play; he exercises with him in the same gymnasium; and all as suits his humor. But at Lacedæmon there is not one man who would not feel ashamed to welcome the coward at the common mess-tables or to try conclusions with such an antagonist in a wrestling bout. Consider the day's round of his existence. The sides are being picked up in a foot-ball match, but he is left out as the odd man; there is no place for him. During the Choric dance he is driven away into ignominious quarters. Nay, in the very streets, it is he who must step aside for others to pass, or, being seated, he must rise and make room even for a younger man. At home he will have his maiden relatives to support in their isolation (and they will hold him to blame for their unwedded lives). A hearth with no wife to bless it—that is the condition he must face—and yet he will have to pay damages to the last farthing for incurring it. Let him not roam abroad with a smooth and smiling countenance; let him not imitate men whose fame is irreproachable, or he shall feel on his back the blows of his superiors; such being the weight of infamy which is laid upon all cowards, I, for my part, am not surprised, if in Sparta they deem death preferable to a life so steeped in dishonor and reproach. (Vol. II, 311-312.)

QUESTIONS.

1. Why does "Salvation attend on virtue (what did the Spartan understand by virtue?) more frequently than on cowardice?" 2. Why should the position of the coward in Sparta differ so much from his position in other states? 3. Give all the reasons why a Spartan preferred to die in battle rather than to flee? 4. How would this treatment help to realize the Spartan ideal?

THE PRACTICE OF EVERY VIRTUE ENFORCED.

That, too, was a happy enactment, in my opinion, by which Lycurgus provided for the continual cultivation of virtues, even to old age. By fixing the election to the Council of Elders as a last ordeal at the goal of life, he made it impossible for a high standard of virtuous living to be disregarded even in old age. (So, too, it is worthy of admiration in him that he lent his helping hand to a virtuous old age. Thus, by making the elders sole arbiters in the trial for life, he contrived to charge old age with a greater weight of honor than that which is accorded to the strength of mature manhood.) And assuredly such a contest as this must appeal to the zeal of mortal man beyond all others in a supreme degree. Fair, doubtless, are contests of gymnastic skill, yet are they trials of but bodily excellence, but this contest for the seniory is of a higher sort—it is an ordeal of the soul itself. In proportion, therefore, as the soul is worthier than the body, so must these contests of the soul appeal to a stronger enthusiasm than their bodily antitypes.

And yet another point may well excite our admiration for Lycurgus largely. It had not escaped his observation that communities exist where those who are willing to make virtue their study and delight fail somehow in ability to add to the glory of the fatherland. That lesson the legislator laid to heart, and in Sparta he enforced, as a matter of public duty, the practice of every virtue by every citizen. And so it is that, just as man differs from man in some excellence, according as he cultivates or neglects to cultivate it, this city of Sparta, with good reason, outshines all other states in virtue; since she, and she alone, has made the attainment of a high standard of noble living a public duty.

And was not this a noble enactment, that whereas other states are content to inflict punishment only in cases where a man does wrong against his neighbor, Lycurgus imposed penalties no less severe on him who openly neglected to make himself as good as possible? For this, it seems, was his principle: in the one case, where a man is robbed, or defrauded, or kidnapped, and made a slave of, the injury of the misdeed, whatever it be, is personal to the individual so maltreated; but in the other case, whole communities suffer foul treason at the hands of a base man and the coward. So that it was only reasonable, in my opinion, that he should visit the heaviest penalty upon these latter.

Moreover, he laid upon them, like some irresistible necessity, the obligation to cultivate the whole virtue of a citizen. Provided they duly perform the injunctions of the law, the city belonged to them each and all, in absolute possession, and on an equal footing. Weakness of limb or want of wealth was no drawback in his eyes. But as for him who, out of the cowardice of his heart, shrank from the painful performance of the law's injunction, the finger of the legislator pointed him out as there and then disqualified to be regarded longer as a member of the brotherhood of peers.

It may be added, that there is no doubt as to the great antiquity of this code of laws. . . . But being of so long standing, these laws, even at this day, still are stamped in the eyes of other men with all of the novelty of youth. And the most marvelous thing of all is that, while everybody is agreed to praise these remarkable institutions, there is not a single state which cares to imitate them. (Vol. II, 312-314.)

QUESTIONS.

1. Explain the relation of the Council of Elders to

the Spartan system. 2. Why was this council made up of old men? 3. What was the highest duty of the Spartan? 4. What do you think of the distinction made by Xenophon between the punishment of a defrauder and a coward? 5. What one thing was required of all men? 6. Why did other states not care to imitate Spartan institutions?

ARMY ORGANIZATION AND MILITARY TACTICS.

The above form a common stock of blessings, open to every Spartan to enjoy, alike in peace and in war. But if any one desires to be informed in what way the legislator improved upon the ordinary machinery of warfare and in reference to an army in the field, it is easy to satisfy his curiosity.

In the first instance, the ephors announce in proclamation the limit of age to which the service applies for cavalry and heavy infantry; and in the next place, for the various handicraft men. So that, even on active service, the Lacedæmonians are well supplied with all the conveniences enjoyed by people living as citizens at home. All the implements and instruments whatsoever, which an army may need in common, are ordered to be in readiness, some on wagons and others on baggage animals. In this way anything omitted can hardly escape detection.

For the actual encounter under arms, the following inventions are attributed to him: The soldier has a crimson colored uniform and a heavy shield of bronze; his theory being that such an equipment has no sort of feminine association, and is altogether most warrior-like. It is most quickly burnished; it is least readily soiled.

He further permitted those who were about the age of early manhood to wear their hair long. For so, he conceived, they would appear of larger statue, more free and indomitable, and of a more terrible aspect.

So furnished and accoutred, he divided his citizen soldiers into six morai (or regimental divisions) of cavalry and heavy infantry. Each of these citizen regiments (political divisions) has one polemarch (or colonel), four lochagoi (or captains of companies), eight pentecontcrs (or lieutenants, each in command of a half company), and sixteen enomotarchs (or commanders of sections). At a word of command any such regimental division can be formed readily either into enomoties (i. e. single file) or into threes (i. e. three files abreast), or into sixes (i. e. six files abreast).

As to the idea, commonly entertained, that the tactical arrangement of the Laconian heavy infantry is highly complicated, no conception could be more opposed to facts. For in the Laconian order the front rank men are all leaders, so that each file has everything necessary to play its part efficiently. In fact, this disposition is so easy to understand that no one who can distinguish one human being from another can fail to follow it. One set have the privilege of leaders, the other the duty of followers. The evolutional orders by which greater depth or shallowness is given to the battle line, are given by word of mouth, by the enomotarch (or commander of the section), and they cannot be mistaken. None of these manœuvers presents any difficulty whatsoever to the understanding. (Vol. II, 314-316.)

QUESTIONS.

1. Did all Spartans perform military service? 2. Was life in the field unpleasant? 3. Prove that in all things the Spartan was practical and his aim to conquer. 4. How many officers in a regiment? 5. Compare the tactics of the Spartan with those of a modern regiment. 6. Were the Spartans superior in tactics to the other Greeks?

MODE OF ENCAMPMENT.

I will now speak of the mode of encampment, sanctioned by the regulation of Lycurgus. To avoid the waste incidental to the angles of the square, the encampment, according to him, should be circular, except where there was the security of a hill or fortification, or where they had a river in the rear. He had sentinels posted during the day along the place of arms and facing inwards; since they are appointed not so much for the sake of the enemy as to keep an eye on friends. The enemy is sufficiently watched by mounted troopers perched on various points commanding the widest prospects.

To guard against hostile approach by night, sentinel duty according to the ordinance was performed by the Sciritæ outside the main body. At the present time the rule is so far modified that the duty is entrusted to foreigners, if there be a foreign contingent present, with a leaven of Spartans to keep them company.

The custom of always taking their spears with them when they go their rounds must certainly be attributed to the same cause which makes them exclude their slaves from a place of arms. . . . The need of precaution is the whole explanation.

The frequency with which they change their encampment is another point. It is done quite as much for the sake of benefiting their friends as annoying their enemies.

Further, the law enjoins upon all Lacedæmonians, during the whole period of an expedition, the constant practice of gymnastic exercises, whereby their pride in themselves is increased, and they appear freer and of a more liberal aspect than the rest of the world. The walk and the running grounds must not exceed in length the space covered by a regimental division, so that one may find himself far from his own stand of arms. After the gymnastic exercises, the senior polemarch gives the order (by herald) to be seated. This serves all the purposes of an inspection. After this the order is given "To get breakfast," and for "the outpost to be relieved." After this, again, come pastimes and relaxations before the evening exercises, after which the herald's cry is heard "To take the evening meal." When they have sung a hymn to the gods to whom the offerings of happy omen have been performed, the final order, "Retire to rest at the place of arms" is given. (Vol. II, 317-319.)

QUESTIONS.

1. Why should the Spartans watch their friends? 2. Had the Spartan military system changed in Xenophon's day? 3. How did they show their ability in handling the allies that camped with them? 4. What proves that the Spartans realized fully the conditions of victory? 5. Describe "a day in camp."

COVENANT BETWEEN KING AND STATE.

I wish to explain with sufficient detail the nature of the covenant between king and state as instituted by Lycurgus; for this, I take it, is the sole type of rule which still preserves the original form in which it was first established; whereas other constitutions will be found either to have been already modified or else to be still undergoing modification at this moment.

Lycurgus laid it down as law that the king shall offer on behalf of the state all public sacrifices, as being himself of divine descent, and whithersoever the state shall dispatch her armies the king shall take the lead.

He granted him to receive honorary gifts of the things offered in sacrifice, and he appointed him choice land in many of the provincial cities, enough to satisfy moderate needs without excess of wealth. And in order that the kings might also encamp and mess in public he appointed them public quarters, and he honored them with a double portion each at the evening meal, not in order that they might actually eat twice as much as others, but that the king might have wherewithal to honor whomsoever he desires. He also granted as a gift to each of the two kings to choose two mess-fellows, which same are called Tuthioi. He also granted them to receive out of every litter of swine one pig, so that the king might never be at a loss for victims if in aught he wished to consult the gods.

Close by the palace a lake affords an unrestricted supply of water; and how useful that is for various purposes they best can tell who lack the luxury. Moreover, all rise from their seats to give place to the king save only that the Ephors rise not from their throne of office. Monthly they exchange oaths, the Ephors in behalf of the state, the king himself in his own behalf. And this is the oath on the king's part: "I will exercise my kingship in accordance with the established laws of the state." And on the part of the state the oath runs: "So long as he (who exercises kingship) shall abide by his oath we will not suffer his kingdom to be shaken." (Vol. II, 319-320.)

QUESTIONS.

1. What peculiar thing did Xenophon note in connection with the Spartan constitution? 2. Could his statement be true? 3. In what way were the kings distinguished from other men? 4. Why? 5. How did the kings use swine in consulting the gods? 6. Why did not the Ephors rise before the king? 7. What kind of a monarchy was the Spartan government?

ALEXANDER'S METHODS OF WARFARE.

CHAPTER IV.

ALEXANDER'S METHODS OF WARFARE.

Arrian: Anabasis of Alexander and Indica. Translated by Edward James Chinnock, M. A., LL. D., New York, 1893.

ARRIAN wrote in the second century of our era, and consequently did not live contemporaneously with the events described. Alexander lived in the fourth century B. C. But although he was not a contemporary of the great Macedonian, Arrian used the best of contemporary records in writing his history. He had before him the accounts of Alexander's campaigns written by his generals, Ptolemy and Aristobulus. Neither of these works exists today. Plutarch and Strabo made use of these writers, Plutarch basing his "Life of Alexander" chiefly upon the account of Aristobulus. The history of the conquest of the Persian Empire (probably to the battle of Arbela) was written by the historian Kallisthenes, who accompanied Alexander in his expedition. The work has been lost, but portions of it have been preserved in the writings of later historians. Polybius (Bk. XII, chaps., 17-22) criticises the account of the battle of Issus given by Kallisthenes, quoting portions of his work. The pilot Nearchus described the voyage of the fleet commanded by himself, from the Indus to the Persian Gulf. Onesikritus, an historian who accompanied Alexander, wrote an account of Alexander's deeds, but too full of romance to be of much value. There were also official accounts and letters of the King; many of those in circulation, however, were undoubtedly forgeries. As Arrian deals largely with military affairs, and as his chief source, Ptolemy, was one of the ablest of Alexander's generals, we can draw from his work the best of first-hand information upon the question of the methods of warfare employed by Alexander.

An excellent exercise would be a comparison of Arrian's descriptions of the different episodes presented in this study with the treatment found in Plutarch's "Life of Alexander." Another valuable exercise would be the making of a list of authorities cited by Plutarch in his "Life of Alexander." Finally, a third exercise would be a comparison of the extracts taken from Arrian with the treatment of the same events in modern school narratives.

Arrian speaks of his method of work in the following words:

I have admitted into my narrative as strictly authentic all the statements relating to Alexander and Philip which Ptolemy, son of Lagus, and Aristobulus, son of Aristobulus, agree in making; and from those statements which differ I have selected that which appears to me the more credible and at the same time the more deserving of record. Different authors have given different accounts of Alexander's actions; and there is no one about whom more have written, or more at variance with each other. But in my opinion, the narratives of Ptolemy and Aristobulus are more worthy of credit than are the rest; Aristobulus, because he served under King Alexander in his expedition, and Ptolemy, not only because he accompanied Alexander in his expedition, but also because, being a king himself, the falsification of facts would have been more disgraceful to him than to any other man Moreover, they are both more worthy of credit, because they compiled their histories after Alexander's death, when neither compulsion was used, nor reward offered them to write anything different from what really occurred. Some statements also made by other writers I have incorporated in my narrative, because they seem to me worthy of mention and not altogether improbable; but I have given them merely as reports of Alexander's proceedings. (Pages 1 and 2.)

QUESTIONS.

1. Do you think that Arrian's rule touching the statements of Ptolemy and Aristobulus was scientifically correct? 2. What do you think of his rule touching other statements? 3. Criticise his reasons for thinking the accounts of the two generals "more worthy of credit than are the rest."

EVOLUTIONS OF THE PHALANX.

Then Alexander drew up his army in such a way that the depth of the phalanx was 120 men; and stationing 200 cavalry on each wing, he ordered them to preserve silence, receiving the word of command quickly. Accordingly he gave the signal to the heavy armed infantry in the first place to hold their spears erect, and then to couch them at the concerted signal; at one time to incline their spears to the right closely locked together, and at another time towards the left. He then set the phalanx itself into quick motion forward, and marched it toward the wings, now to the right and then to the left. After thus arranging and rearranging his lines many times very rapidly, he at last formed his phalanx into a sort of wedge, and led it toward the left against the enemy, who had long been in a state of amazement at seeing both the order and rapidity of his evolutions. Consequently, they did not sustain Alexander's attack, but quitted the first ridges of the mountain. Upon this, Alexander ordered the Macedonians to raise the battle cry and make clatter with their spears upon their shields, and the Taulantians, being still more alarmed at the noise, led their army back to the city with all speed. (Pages 16 and 17.)

QUESTIONS.

1. How many men in each file of the phalanx? 2. Why did Alexander command silence? 3. What did a soldier do when he "couched" his spear? 4. What is the meaning of the expression "marched toward the wings"? 5. What relation between "couching" the spear and marching toward the wings? 6. Were Alexander's troops better trained than the enemy? 7. Why does Alexander at one time command silence and at another order his men to make a noise? 8. Make a diagram of the operations described by Arrian.

BATTLE OF ISSUS.

Having thus marshalled his men, he caused them to rest for some time, and then led them forward, as he had resolved that their advance should be very slow. For Darius was no longer leading the foreigners against him as he had arranged them at first, but he remained in his position upon the bank of the river, which was in many parts steep and precipitous; and in certain places, where it seemed more easy to ascend, he extended a stockade along it. By this it was at once evident to Alexander's men that Darius had become cowed in spirit. But when the armies were at length close to each other, Alexander rode about in every direction to exhort his troops to show their valor, mentioning with befitting epithets the names, not only of the generals, but also those of the captains of cavalry and infantry and of the Grecian mercenaries as many as were distinguished either by reputation or any deed of valor. From all sides arose a shout not to delay, but to attack the enemy. At first he still led them on in close array with measured step, although he had the forces of Darius already in distant view, lest by a too hasty march any part of the phalanx should fluctuate from the lines and get separated from the rest. But when they came within range of darts, Alexander himself and those around him, being posted on the right wing, dashed first into the river with a run, in order to alarm the Persians by the rapidity of their onset, and by coming sooner to close conflict to avoid being much injured by the archers. And it turned out just as Alexander had conjectured; for as soon as the battle became a hand to hand one, the part of the Persian army stationed on the left wing were put to route; and here Alexander and his men won a brilliant victory. But the Grecian mercenaries serving under Darius attacked the Macedonians at the point where they saw their phalanx especially disordered. For the Macedonian phalanx had been broken and had disjoined towards the right wing; because Alexander had dashed into the river with eagerness, and engaging in a hand to hand conflict, was already driving back the Persians posted there; but the Macedonians in the center had not prosecuted their task with equal eagerness, and finding many parts of the bank steep and precipitous, they were unable to preserve the front of the phalanx in the same line. Here, then, the struggle was desperate; the Grecian mercenaries of Darius fighting in order to push the Macedonians back into the river, and regain the victory for their allies who were already flying; the Macedonians struggling in order not to fall short of Alexander's success, which was already manifest, and not to tarnish the glory of the phalanx, which up to that time had been commonally proclaimed invincible. Moreover, the feeling of rivalry which existed between the Grecian and Macedonian races inspired each side in the conflict. Here fell Ptolemy, son of Seleucus, after proving himself a valiant man, besides about one hundred and twenty Macedonians of no mean repute.

Hereupon the regiments on the right wing, perceiving that the Persians opposed to them had already been put to route, wheeled around towards the Grecian mercenaries of Darius and their own hard pressed detachment. Having driven the Greeks away from the river, they extended their phalanx beyond the Persian army on the side which had been broken; and attacking the Greeks on the flank were already beginning to cut them up. However, the Persian cavalry, which had been posted opposite the Thessalians, did not remain on the other side of the river during the struggle, but came through the water and made a vigorous attack upon the Thessalian squadrons. In this place a fierce cavalry battle ensued; for the Persians did not give way until they perceived that Darius had fled and the Grecian mercenaries had been cut up by the phalanx and severed from them. Then, at last, there ensued a decided flight, and on all sides. (Pages 88-92.)

QUESTIONS.

1. Enumerate all the characteristics of a good commander shown by Alexander during the struggle at Issus, and state the value of each. 2. Why should Alexander's men think that Darius' men were cowards in spirit because they built a stockade? 3. Was not the sudden dash made by Alexander a daring and dangerous move? 4. Did it show good generalship? 5. Where did the Macedonians encounter the most resistance? 6. To what was the victory of the Macedonians due? 7. Make a diagram of the movements described.

SIEGE OF GAZA.

Gaza is about twenty stades (two miles and a half) from the sea; the approach to it is sandy and the sand deep, and the sea near the city everywhere shallow. The city of Gaza was large and had been built upon a lofty mound, around which a strong wall had been carried. It is the last city the traveler meets with going from Phœnicia to Egypt, being situated on the edge of the desert. When Alexander arrived near the city, on the first day he encamped at the spot where the walls seemed to him most easy for him to assail, and ordered his military engines to be constructed. But the engineers expressed the opinion that it was not possible to capture the wall by force, on account of the height of the mound. However, the more impracticable it seemed to be, the more resolutely Alexander determined that it must be captured. For, he said, that the action would strike the enemy with great alarm from its being contrary to their expectation; whereas, his failure to capture the place would redound to his disgrace when mentioned either to the Greeks or to Darius. He therefore resolved to construct a mound right around the city, so as to be able to bring his military engines up to the walls on the same level on the artificial mound which had been raised. The mound was constructed especially over against the southern wall of the city, where it appeared easiest to make an assault. When he thought that the mound had been raised to the proper level with the walls, the Macedonians placed their military engines upon it and brought them close to the walls of Gaza. At this time, while Alexander was offering sacrifice, and, crowned with a garland, was about to commence the first sacred rite according to custom, a certain carnivorous bird, flying over the altar, let a stone, which it was carrying with its claws, fall upon his head. Alexander asked Aristander, the soothsayer, what this omen meant. He replied: "O, king, thou wilt indeed capture the city, but thou must take care of thyself on this day."

When Alexander heard this he kept himself for a time near the military engines, out of the reach of missiles. But when a vigorous sortie was made from the city, and the Arabs were carrying torches to set fire to the military engines, and from their commanding position above hurling missiles at the Macedonians, who were defending themselves from lower ground, were driving them down from the mound, which they had made, then Alexander either wilfully disobeyed the soothsayer, or forgot the prophecy from excitement in the heat of action. Taking the shield-bearing guards, he hastened to the rescue where the Macedonians were especially hard pressed, and prevented them from being driven down from the mound in disgraceful flight. But he was himself wounded by a bolt from a catapult, right through the shield and breast-plate into the shoulder. When he perceived that Aristander had spoken the truth about the wound he rejoiced, because he thought he should also capture the city by the aid of the soothsayer. And yet, indeed, he was not easily cured of the wound. In the meantime, the military engines with which he had captured Tyre arrived, having been sent for by sea; and he ordered the mound to be constructed quite around the city on all sides, two stades* in breadth, and 250 feet in height. When his engines had been prepared and brought up along the mound, they shook down a large extent of wall; and mines being dug in various places and the earth being drawn out by stealth, the wall fell down in many parts, subsiding into the empty space. The Macedonians then commanded a large extent of ground with their missiles, driving back the men who were defending the city from the towers. Nevertheless, the men of the city sustained three assaults, though many of their number were killed or wounded; but at the fourth attack Alexander led up the phalanx of the Macedonians from all sides, threw down the part of the wall which was undermined, and shook down another large portion of it by battering it with his engines, so that he rendered the assault an easy matter through the breaches with his scaling ladders. Accordingly the ladders were brought up to the wall; and then there arose a great emulation among those of the Macedonians who laid any claim to valor to see who should be the first to scale the walls. The first to do so was Neoptolemus, one of the Companions, of the family of the Æacidæ; and after him mounted one rank after another with their officers. When once some of the Macedonians got within the wall they split open in

---

*A stadium equalled 606¼ feet.

succession the gates which each party happened to light upon, and thus admitted the whole army into the city. But though the city was now in the hands of the enemy, the Gazæans nevertheless stood together and fought; so that they were all slain fighting there as each man had been stationed. Alexander sold their wives and children into slavery; and having peopled the city again from the neighboring settlers, he made use of it as a fortified post for the war. (Pages 124-127.)

QUESTIONS.

1. Does Alexander's refusal to accept the opinion of his engineers show his greatness or his foolhardiness? 2. Do you consider his reasons for undertaking the siege sufficient? 3. What were the military engines? 4. What purposes did they serve? 5. What was the object of the "sacred rite"? 6. Describe the means by which a walled city was taken. 7 Why were Alexander's soldiers so enthusiastic?

THE PURSUIT OF DARIUS.

At this time Bagistanes, one of the Babylonian nobles, came to him from the camp of Darius, accompanied by Antibelus, one of the sons of Mazæus. These men informed him that Nabarzanes, the commander of the cavalry which accompanied Darius in his flight; Bessus, viceroy of the Bactrians, and Barsaentes, viceroy of the Arachotians and Drangians, had arrested the king. When Alexander heard this he marched with still greater speed than ever, taking with him only the Companions and the skirmishing cavalry, as well as some of the foot soldiers, selected as the strongest and lightest men. . . His own men took with them nothing but their arms and provisions for two days. After marching the whole night until noon of the next day, he gave his army a short rest, then went on again all night, and when day began to break reached the camp from which Bagistanes had set out to meet him; but he did not catch the enemy. However, in regard to Darius, he ascertained that he had been arrested and was being conveyed in a covered carriage; that Bessus possessed the command instead of Darius. . . . He also learned that those who had arrested Darius had come to the decision to surrender him to Alexander and to procure some advantage for themselves, if they should find that Alexander were pursuing them. . . .

Hearing this, Alexander thought it necessary to pursue with all his might; and though his men and horses were already quite fatigued by the incessant severity of their labors, he nevertheless proceeded, and, traveling a long way all through the night and the next day till noon, arrived at a certain village, where those who were leading Darius had encamped the day before. Hearing there that the barbarians had decided to continue their march by night, he inquired of the natives if they knew any shorter road to the fugitives. They said they did know one, but it ran through a country which was desert through lack of water. He nevertheless ordered them to show him this way, and perceiving that the infantry could not keep up with him if he marched at full speed, he caused 500 of the cavalry to dismount from their horses, and selecting the officers of the infantry and the best of the other foot soldiers, he ordered them to mount the horses armed just as they were. He also directed Nicanor, the commander of the shield-bearing guards, and Attalus, commander of the Agrianians, to lead their men who were left behind by the same route which Bessus had taken, having equipped them as lightly as possible; and he ordered the rest of the infantry to follow in regular marching order. He himself began to march in the afternoon, and led the way with great rapidity. Having traveled 400 stades (about 47 miles) in the night, he came upon the barbarians just before daybreak, going along without any order and unarmed; so that only a few of them rushed to defend themselves, but most of them, as soon as they saw Alexander himself, took to flight without even coming to blows. A few of those who had turned to resist being killed, the rest of these also took to flight. Up to this time, Bessus and his party were still conveying Darius with them in a covered carriage; but when Alexander was already close upon them, Nabarzanes and Barsaentes wounded him and left him there, and with six hundred horsemen took to flight. Darius died from his wounds soon after, before Alexander had seen him. (Pages 168-170.)

QUESTIONS.

1. In what way did Alexander show his superior generalship in the pursuit of Darius? 2. Why did he march his forces in three divisions? 3. What proof

does this extract give that Alexander was capable of great endurance?

CAPTURE OF THE SOGDIAN ROCK.

If this rock was captured, it seemed that nothing would any longer be left to those of the Sogdians who wished to throw off their allegiance. When Alexander approached it he found it precipitous on all sides against assault, and that the barbarians had collected provisions for a long siege. The great quantity of snow which had fallen helped to make the assault more difficult to the Macedonians, while at the same time it kept the barbarians supplied with plenty of water. But notwithstanding all this, he resolved to assault the place; for a certain overweening and insolent boast uttered by the barbarians had thrown him into a wrathful state of ambitious pertinacity. For when they were invited to come to terms of capitulation, and it was held out to them as an inducement that if they surrendered the place they would be allowed to withdraw with safety to their abodes, they burst out laughing, and in their barbaric tongue bade Alexander seek winged soldiers to capture the mountain for him, since they had no apprehension of danger from other men. He then issued a proclamation that the first man who mounted should have a reward of twelve talents,* the man who came next to him the second prize, and the third so on in proportion, so that the last reward should be 300 darics,† to the last prize-taker who reached the top. This proclamation excited the ardor of the Macedonians still more, though they were even before very ready to commence the assault.

All the men who had gained practice in scaling rocks in sieges banded themselves together to the number of three hundred, and provided themselves with small iron pegs with which their tents had been fastened to the ground, with the intention of fixing them into the snow, wherever it might be seen to be frozen hard, or into the ground if it should anywhere exhibit itself free from snow. Tieing strong ropes made of flax to these pegs, they advanced to the most precipitous part of the rock, which was on this account most unguarded; and fixing some of these pegs into the earth where it made itself visible, and others into the snow where it seemed

---

* About $14,000.   † About $1,500.

least likely to crumble, they hoisted themselves up the rock, some in one place and some in another. Thirty of them perished in the ascent, and as they fell into various parts of the snow, not even could their bodies be found for burial. The rest, however, reached the top of the mountain at the approach of dawn; and, taking possession of it, they waved linen flags towards the camp of the Macedonians, as Alexander had directed them to do. He now sent a herald with instructions to shout to the sentries of the barbarians to make no further delay, but to surrender at once, since the "winged men" had been found, and the summits of the mountain were in their possession. At the same time the herald pointed to the soldiers upon the crest of the mountain. The barbarians, being alarmed by the unexpectedness of the sight, and suspecting that the men who were occupying the peaks were more numerous than they really were, and that they were completely armed, surrendered, so frightened did they become at the sight of those few Macedonians. (Pages 220-222.)

QUESTIONS.

1. Why did Alexander attack the Sogdian Rock? 2. Enumerate the obstacles that would have appeared insuperable to the ordinary man. 3. Name the conditions that made it possible for Alexander to succeed. 4. How many of the conditions were under his control? 5. How does this incident show his great insight into human nature?

ALEXANDER WOUNDED.

On the following day, dividing the army into two parts, he himself assaulted the wall at the head of one and Perdiccas led on the other. Upon this the Indians did not wait to receive the attack of the Macedonians, but abandoned the walls of the city and fled for safety into the citadel. Alexander and his troops, therefore, split open a small gate, and got within the city long before the others; for those who had been put under Perdiccas were behind time, having experienced difficulty in scaling the walls, as most of them did not bring ladders, thinking that the city had been captured, when they observed that the walls were deserted by the defenders. But when the citadel was seen to be still in possession of the enemy, and many of them were observed drawn up in front of it to repel the attacks, some of the Macedonians tried to force an entry by undermining the wall, and others by placing scaling ladders against it wherever it was practicable to do so. Alexander, thinking that the men who carried the ladders were too slow, snatched one from a man who was carrying it, placed it against the wall himself, and began to mount it, crouching under his shield. After him mounted Peucestas, the man who carried the sacred shield which Alexander took from the temple of the Trojan Athena, and used to keep with him and have it carried before him in all his battles. After Peucestas, by the same ladder, ascended Leonnatus, the confidential body guard; and up another ladder went Abreas, one of the soldiers who received double pay for distinguished services. The king was now near the battlement of the walls, and leaning his shield against it was pushing some of the Indians within the fort, and had cleared that part of the wall by killing others with his sword. The shield-bearing guards, becoming very anxious for the king's safety, pushed themselves with ardor up the same ladder and broke it; so that those who were already mounting fell down and made the ascent impractical for the rest. Alexander, then, standing upon the walls, was being assailed all around from the adjacent towers; for none of the Indians dared to approach him. He was also being assailed by the men in the city, who were throwing darts at him from no great distance; for a mound of earth happened to have been heaped up there opposite the walls. Alexander was conspicuous both by the brilliancy of his weapons and by his extraordinary display of audacity. He therefore perceived that if he remained where he was he would be incurring danger without being able to perform anything at all worthy of consideration; but if he leaped down within the fort he might, perhaps, by this very act strike the Indians with terror, and if he did not, but should only thereby be incurring danger, and at any rate he would die not ignobly after performing great deeds of valor worth hearing about by men of after times. Forming this resolution, he leaped down from the wall into the citadel; where, supporting himself against the wall, he struck with his sword and killed some of the Indians who came to close quarters with him, including their leader, who rushed upon him too boldly. Another man who approached him he kept in check by hurling a stone at him, and a third in like manner. Another, who had advanced nearer to him, he again kept off with his sword; so that the barbarians were no longer willing to approach him, but standing around him, cast at him from all sides whatever missile any one happened to have or could get hold of at the time.

Meantime, Peucestas and Arbreas, the soldier entitled to double pay, and after them Leonnatus, being the only men who happened to have scaled the walls before the ladders were broken, had leaped down and were fighting in front of the king. Arbreas, the man entitled to double pay, fell there, being shot with an arrow in the forehead. Alexander, himself, also was wounded with an arrow under the breast, through his breastplate in the chest, so that, Ptolemy says, air was breathed out from the wound together with the blood. But although he was faint from exhaustion, he defended himself as long as his blood was still warm. But the blood streaming out copiously and without ceasing at every expiration of breath, he was seized with a dizziness and swooning, and bending over, fell upon his shield. After he had fallen, Peucestas defended him, holding over him in front the sacred shield brought from Troy; and on the other side he was defended by Leonnatus. But both these men were themselves wounded, and Alexander was now nearly fainting away from loss of blood. For the Macedonians had experienced great difficulty in the assault also on this account, because those who saw Alexander being shot at upon the walls, and then leaping down into the citadel within, in their ardor arising from fear lest their king should meet with any mishap by recklessly exposing himself to danger, broke the ladders. Then some began to devise one plan and others another to mount upon the walls, as well as they could in their state of embarrassment, some fixing pegs into the wall, which was made of earth, and suspending themselves from these, hoisted themselves up with difficulty by their means; others got up by mounting one upon the other. The first who got up threw himself down from the wall into the city, and so did they all, with a loud lamentation and howl of grief, when they saw the king lying on the ground. Now ensued a desperate conflict around the fallen body, one Macedonian after another holding his shield in front of him. In the meantime some of the soldiers having shivered in pieces the bar by which the gate in the space of the wall between the towers was secured, entered the city a few at a time; while others, putting their shoulders under the gap made by the gate, forced their way into the space inside the wall, and thus laid the citadel open in that quarter.

Hereupon some of them began to kill the Indians, all of whom they slew, sparing not even a woman or child. Others carried off the king, who was lying in a faint condition upon his shield; and they could not yet tell whether he was likely to survive. (Pages 306-309.)

QUESTIONS.

1. What was the relation of the citadel to the city? 2. Why did Alexander crouch under his shield on mounting the ladder? 3. What were the battlements? 4. What was evidently the duty of the three men that accompanied Alexander? 5. Who were the bodyguards? 6. Why was Alexander's position dangerous? 7. Why did he not jump outside the wall? 8. In what ways did the soldiers show their excellent training? 9. What was the great defect? 10. Why were the women and children killed?

ALEXANDER'S RECOVERY.

When the ship bearing the king approached the camp he ordered the tent covering to be removed from the stern that he might be visible to all. But they were still incredulous, thinking, forsooth, that Alexander's corpse was being conveyed on the vessel; until at length he stretched out his hand to the multitude when the ship was nearing the bank. Then the men raised a cheer, lifting their hands, some toward the sky, and others to the king himself. Many even shed involuntary tears at the unexpected sight. Some of the shieldbearing guards brought a litter for him when he was conveyed out of the ship; but he ordered them to fetch his horse. When he was seen again mounting his horse, the whole army re-echoed with loud clapping of hands, so that the banks of the river and the groves near them reverberated with the sound. On approaching his tent he dismounted from his horse, so that he might be seen walking. Then the men came near, some on one side, some on the other, some touching his hands, others his knees, others only his clothes. Some only came close enough to get a sight of him, and went away having chanted his praise, while others threw garlands upon him of the flowers which the country of Indian supplied at that season of the year. Nearchus says that some of his friends incurred his displeasure reproaching him for exposing himself to danger in the front of the army in battle; which, they said, was the duty of the private soldier and not that of the general. (Page 313.)

QUESTIONS.

1. Why were the soldiers so incredulous about the recovery of Alexander? 2. Why did they cheer and weep? 3. Why did Alexander prefer the horse to the litter? 4. Why did the soldiers want to touch Alexander? 5. What do you think of the remark made by Alexander's friends? 6. Make an outline and write a narrative upon the subject of this whole study, citing evidence in support of all statements.

THE ACHAEAN LEAGUE.

CHAPTER V.

THE ACHAEAN LEAGUE.

Polybius: The Histories of Polybius. Translated from the text of F. Hultsch by Evelyn S. Schuckburgh, M. A. 2 vols. New York, 1889.

"POLYBIUS, of Megalopolis, was the son of Lycortas, the friend and partisan of Philopoemen, who had served the Achaean league in several capacities." Polybius was born about 203 B. C., and died about 121 B. C. He lived in the midst of the events that he described, and "wrote with even more complete personal knowledge than Thucydides," who described the Peloponnesian war in which he took part. "Not only was Polybius the son of a man who had held the highest office in the league, and so must have heard the politics and history of Achaia discussed from his earliest youth; not only from early manhood was he himself in the thick of political business, but he knew the sovereigns of Egypt and Pergamus, of Macedonia and Syria, and the Roman generals who conquered the latter." In the extracts that follow, Polybius refers to himself as ambassador and also refers to a speech made by himself in the assembly. He was one of the thousand prominent Achaeans sent to Italy in 167 B. C., and passed sixteen years in Rome, where he became the tutor of the sons of Aemilius Paulus, the Roman general. In 146 B. C. he was in Africa with Scipio, saw the destruction of Carthage, and heard Scipio exclaim: "O, Polybius; it is a grand thing, but, I know not how, I feel a terror and dread, lest someone should one day give the same order about my own native city."

The historian was well prepared for his work: he was himself a participant in the affairs described and by his connections was able to secure the most reliable information touching the things that did not pass under his own eyes. Concerning the organization and working of the league, he could speak from experience, and as our extracts practically deal with nothing else, this is probably the most reliable material that has yet appeared in the Studies.

The Achaean league was the one promising effort made by the Greeks to introduce representative government. It is one of the very few federal governments that have existed in the world's history and for that reason this study is of the utmost concern to the sons and daughters of the greatest of federal governments.

CHARACTER OF THE LEAGUE.

The Achaeans, as I have stated before, have in our time made extraordinary progress in material prosperity and internal unity. For though many statesmen had tried in past times to induce the Peloponnesians to join in a common league for the common interests of all, and had always failed, because everyone was working to secure his own power rather than the freedom of the whole; yet in our day this policy has made such progress, and been carried out with such completeness, that not only is there in the Peloponnese a community of interests such as exists between allies or friends, but an absolute identity of laws, weights, measures, and currency. All the States have the same magistrates, senate, and judges. Nor is there any difference between the entire Peloponnese and a single city, except in the fact that its inhabitants are not included within the same wall; in other respects, both as a whole and in their individual cities, there is a nearly absolute assimilation of institutions. (II, 37.)

QUESTIONS.

1. At what time was the league in a prosperous condition? 2. Who belonged to the league? 3. What does Polybius mean by "a nearly absolute assimilation of institutions"? 4. Enumerate the institutions that the states had in common and state what benefit they would derive from each one. 5. Why did the league succeed in Polybius' day?

THE OFFICERS AND THEIR POWERS.

With this purpose, he persuaded Philip to be at Aegium at the time of the Achaean election, on the pretext of being on his way to Elis. The king's consent to this enabled Appelles himself to be there at the right time, and though he found great difficulty, in spite of the entreaties and threats, in carrying this point, yet he dd eventually succeed in getting Eperatus of Pharae elected Strategus, and Timoxenus, the candidate proposed by Aratus, rejected. (IV, 82.)

QUESTIONS.

1. What was the chief officer of the league called? 2. How do you know that he was the chief officer? (Use following extracts.) 3. How did he obtain his office? 4. What bad influences do you see at work in connection with the election?

Dorimachus and Scopas waited until Timoxenus had a very short time of office left, and when Aratus, though elected by the Achaeans for the coming year, would not yet be in office. (IV, 6.)

QUESTIONS.

1. What office did Timoxenus hold? 2. How long did he serve? (See other extracts.) 3. Did a man begin to serve as soon as elected?

The year of office as Strategus of the younger Aratus had now come to an end with the rising of the Pleiades*; for that was the arrangement of time then observed by the Achaeans. Accordingly he laid down his office and was succeeded in the command of the Achaeans by Eperatus. (V, 1.)

QUESTION.

1. What right had Eperatus to succeed Aratus?

Having landed at Naupactus, Flaminius addressed a dispatch to the Strategus and Demiurgi† bidding them

---
*May 13.
†Ten federal magistrates.

summon the Achaeans to an assembly; to which they wrote back that "they would do so if he would write them word what the subjects were on which he wished to confer with the Achaeans; for the laws enjoined that limitation on the magistrates." (XXIII, 5.)

QUESTIONS.

1. Who had the power to summon an assembly? 2. Find other references to the Demiurgi (not by name). 4. Under what conditions could the magistrates summon an assembly?

When the ambassadors arrived in Sparta with their answer the Achaean Strategus, as soon as he had settled the Messenian business, summoned a congress at Sicyon, and on its assembling, proposed a resolution for the reception of Sparta into the league. (XXIII, 17.)

QUESTIONS.

1. What powers of the Strategus are shown by this extract? 2. Who had power to admit new members into the league?

THE COUNCIL.

The Achaean Strategus, having summoned his colleagues to council, and given the envoys a hearing, answered. (XXIII, 16.)

QUESTIONS.

(Compare this extract with the preceding.) 1. Who were these colleagues of the Strategus? 2. What purpose did they serve? 3. What kind of business was transacted here?

THE ASSEMBLY.

In the Peloponnesus a mission arrived before the end of the winter from the two kings, Ptolemy (Philometor) and Ptolemy (Physcon), asking for help. . . . The ambassadors arrived when the Achaean congress was in session in Corinth. They therefore came forward and, after recalling the many evidences of friendship shown by the Achaeans to the kingdom of Egypt and describing to them the danger in which the kings then were, they entreated them to send help. The Achaeans generally were ready enough to go to the help of the kings (for both now wore the diadem and exercised regal. functions), and not only with a detachment, but with their full levy. (XXIX, 23.)

QUESTIONS.

1. Over what countries were these kings ru'ers? 2. Were they at war with each other? 3. What was the regular place of assembly for the league? 4. What is meant by the "full levy"? 5. Why should the Achaeans help the kings?

This being the time, according to their laws, for the meeting of the Achaean federal assembly, the members arrived at Aegium. When the assembly met, the deputies from Patrae and Pharae made a formal statement of the injuries inflicted upon their territories during the passage of the Aetolians; an embassy from Messenia also appeared, begging for their assistance on the ground that the treatment from which they were suffering was unjust and in defiance of treaty. . . . Roused to indignation by all these considerations, the assembly voted to give assistance to the Messenians; that the Strategus should summon a general levy of the Achaean arms; and that whatever was decided by this levy, when it met, should be done. Now Timoxenus, the existing Strategus, was just on the point of quitting office, and felt besides small confidence in the Achaeans, because martial exercise had been allowed to fall into neglect among them; he therefore shrank from undertaking the expedition, or from even summoning the popular levy. (IV, 7.)

QUESTIONS.

1. How often and at what time did the assembly meet? 2. Enumerate the powers exercised by the assembly in this extract. 3. What defects in the government are shown?

I have already stated that in the Peloponnese, while Philopoemen was still Strategus, the Achaean league sent an embassy to Rome on the subject of Sparta, and another to King Ptolemy to renew their ancient alliance.

Immediately after Philopoemen had been succeeded by Aristaenus as Strategus the ambassadors of King Ptolemy arrived, while the league meeting was assembled at Megalopolis. King Eumenes also had dispatched an embassy offering to give the Achaeans one hundred and twenty talents on condition that it was invested and the interest used to pay the council of the league at the time of the federal assemblies.

Ambassadors came also from King Seleucus to renew his friendship with them, and offering a present of a fleet of ten ships of war. But when the assembly got to business the first to come forward to speak was Nicodemus of Elis, who recounted to the Achaeans what he and his colleagues had said in the Senate about Sparta, and read the answer of the Senate, which was to the effect that the Senate disapproved of the destruction of the walls, and of the execution of the men put to death at Compasium, and that it did not rescind any arrangement made. No one saying a word for or against this, the subject was allowed to pass.

Next came the ambassadors from Eumenes, who renewed the ancestral friendship of the king with the Achaeans, and stated to the assembly the offer made by him. They spoke at great length on these subjects and retired after setting forth the greatness of the king's kindness and affection to the nation. (XXII, 10.)

After they had finished their speech, Apollonidas of Sicyon rose and said that: "As far as the amount of the money was concerned, it was a present worthy of the Achaeans. But if they looked to the intention of the donor, or the purpose to which the gift was to be applied, none could well be more insulting and more unconstitutional. The laws prohibited any one, whether a private individual or magistrate, from accepting presents from a king on any pretense whatever; but if they took this money they would every one of them be plainly accepting a present, which was at once the greatest possible breach of the law, and confessedly the deepest possible personal disgrace. For that the council should take a great wage from Eumenes, and meet to deliberate on the interests of the league after swallowing such a bait was manifestly disgraceful and injurious. It was Eumenes that offered money now; presently it would be Prusias; and then Seleucus. But as the interests of democracies and kings are quite opposite to each other, and as our most frequent and most important deliberations concern the points of controversy arising between us and the kings, one of two things must necessarily happen; either the interests of the king will have precedence over our own or we must incur the reproach of ingratitude for opposing our paymasters." He therefore urged the Achaeans not only to decline the offer, but to hold Eumenes in detestation for thinking of making it. . . .

After these speeches had been delivered the people showed such signs of enthusiastic approval that no one ventured to speak on the side of the king; but the whole assembly rejected the offer by acclamation, though its amount made it exceedingly tempting. (XXII, 11.)

The next subject introduced for debate was that of King Ptolemy. The ambassadors who had been on the mission to Ptolemy were called forward, and Lycortas, acting as spokesman, began by stating how they had interchanged oaths of alliance with the king; and next announced that they brought a present from the king to the Achaean league of six thousand stands of arms for peltasts, and two thousand talents in bronze coinage. He added a panegyric on the king and finished his speech by a brief reference to the good will and active benevolence of the king towards the Achaeans. Upon this the Strategus of the Achaeans, Aristaenus, stood up and asked Lycortas and his colleagues in the embassy to Ptolemy "which alliance it was that he had thus renewed?"

No one answering the question, but all the assembly beginning to converse with each other, the council chamber was filled with confusion. The cause of this absurd state of things was this: There had been several treaties of alliance formed between the Achaeans and Ptolemy's kingdom, as widely different in their provision as in the circumstances which gave rise to them; but neither had Ptolemy's envoy made any distinction when arranging for the renewal, merely speaking in general terms on the matter, nor had the ambassadors sent from Achaia; but they had interchanged the oaths on the assumption of there being but one treaty. The result was that, on the Strategus quoting all the treaties, and pointing out in detail the differences between them, which turned out to be important, the assembly demanded to know which it was that it was renewing. And when no one was able to explain, not even Philopoemen himself, who had been in office when the renewal was made, nor Lycortas and his colleagues, who had been on the mission to Alexandria, these men all began to be regarded as careless in conducting the business of the league; while Aristaenus acquired great reputation as being the only man who knew what he was talking about; and finally the assembly refused to allow the ratification, voting, on account of this blunder, that the business should be postponed.

Then the ambassadors from Seleucus entered with their proposal. The Achaeans, however, voted to renew the friendship with Seleucus, but to decline for the present the gift of the ships.

Having thus finished their deliberations, the assembly broke up, and the people separated to their several cities. (XXII, 12.)

QUESTIONS.

1. How did the league communicate with other states? 2. Why did the kings offer presents to the Achaeans? 3. Who composed the council? 4. What two objections were made to receiving the presents of Eumenes? 5. Were they sound? 6. What were oaths of alliance? 7. How had the Achaean ambassadors shown their incompetence? 8. What power of the assembly shown here? 9. Why were not the presents of Seleucus treated in the same way as those of Eumenes? 10. Enumerate the steps in the making of an alliance.

The people were once more inclined to grant the aid when they heard this; but Callicrates and his party managed to prevent the decree being passed by staggering the magistrates with the assertion that it was unconstitutional to discuss the question of sending help abroad in public assembly. But a short time afterwards a meeting was summoned at Sicyon which was attended not only by the members of the council, but by all citizens over thirty years of age; and after a lengthened debate, Polybius especially dwelling on the fact that the Romans did not require assistance,—in which he was believed not to be speaking without good reason, as he had spent the previous summer in Macedonia at the headquarters of Marcus Philippus,—and also alleging that even supposing the Romans did turn out to require their active support, the Achaeans would not be rendered incapable of furnishing it by the two hundred horse and one thousand foot which were to be sent to Alexandria,—for they could, without any inconvenience, put thirty or forty thousand men into the field,—the majority of the meeting were convinced, and were inclined to the idea of sending the aid. Accordingly, on the second of the two days on which, according to the laws, those who wished to do so were bound to bring forward their motions, Lycortas and Polybius proposed that the aid should be sent. (XXIX, 24.)

Archon, however, the Strategus, rose to support the envoys,—for it was a matter that called for an expression of opinion from the Strategus,—but after a few words he stood down, afraid of being thought to be giving his advice from interested motives and the hope of making money, because he had spent a large sum on his office. Amidst a general feeling of doubt and hesitation, Polybius rose and delivered a long speech. But that part of it which best fell in with the feelings of the populace was that in which he showed that "The original decree of the Achaeans in regard to these honours enacted that such honours as were improper and contrary to law were to be abolished, but not all honours by any means. (XXVIII, 7.)

QUESTIONS.

1. Name all the states with which the Achaeans had foreign relations. 2. Describe the character of these relations. 3. Who were "the magistrates"? 4. Was Callicrates' statement correct? 5. Of whom was the assembly composed? 6. Who had a right to propose measures? 7. At what time? 8. What indication do you find of the strength of the league? 9. Did the Strategus preside over the assembly? 10. How could Archon make money by speaking?

The resolutions passed by the Achaean federal assembly were these: That embassies should be sent to Epirus, Boeotia, Phocis, Acarnania, and Philip to declare how the Aetolians, in defiance of treaty, had twice entered Achaia with arms, and to call upon them for assistance in virtue of their agreement, and for their consent to the admission of the Messenians into the alliance. Next, that the Strategus of the Achaeans should enroll five thousand foot and five hundred horse and support the Messenians in case the Aetolians were to invade their territory, and to arrange with the Lacedaemonians and Messenians how many horse and foot were to be supplied by them severally for the service of the league. (IV, 15.)

QUESTIONS.

1. What kind of business is the assembly transacting here? 2. Were the Messenians and Lacedaemonians members of the league? 3. Why should the league expect help of the states mentioned above? 4. What powers of the Strategus are shown above?

THE ARMY AND NAVY.

After arranging this settlement, Aratus broke up his camp, and going on himself to the congress of the Achaeans, handed over the mercenaries to Lycus of Pharae, as the Sub-Strategus of the league. . . . About the same time the Navarch of the league, having gone on an expedition to Molycria, returned with nearly a hundred captives. Returning once more to Aetolia, he sailed to Chalceia and captured two warships, with their crews, which put out to resist him; and took also a long boat, with its men, on the Aetolian Rhium. There being thus an influx of booty both by sea and land at the same period, and a considerable amount of money and provisions being obtained from this, the soldiers felt confident of getting their pay, and the cities of the league were sanguine of not being likely to be hard pressed by their contributions. (V, 94.)

QUESTIONS.

1. What other officers in the league besides the Strategus? 2. What bad features appear in the organization of the army? 3. How was it supported?

About the same time Euripidas, who had been sent out to act as general to the Eleans, after overrunning the districts of Dyme, Pharae, and Tritaea, and collecting a considerable amount of booty, was marching back to Elis. But Miccus of Dyme, who happened at the time to be Sub-Strategus of the Achaean league, went out to the rescue with a body of Dymaeans, Pharaeans, and Tritaeans, and attacked him as he was returning. (IV, 59.)

Being then appointed Hipparch by the Achaean league at this time, and finding the squadrons in a state of utter demoralization and the men thoroughly dispirited, he did not only restore them to a better state than they were, but in a short time made them even superior to the enemy's cavalry by bringing them all to adopt habits of real training and genuine emulation. The fact is that most of those who hold this office of Hipparch, either, from being without any genius themselves for cavalry tactics, do not venture to enforce necessary orders upon others; or, because they are aiming at being elected Strategus, try all through their year of office to attach the young men to themselves and to secure their favor in the coming election; and accordingly never administer necessary reprimands, which are the salvation of the public interests, but hush up all transgressions, and, for the sake of gaining an insignificant popularity, do great damage to those who trust them. Sometimes, again, commanders, though neither feeble nor corrupt, do more damage to the soldiers by intemperate zeal than the negligent ones, and this is still oftener the case with regard to the cavalry. . . . (X, 22.)

QUESTIONS.

1. What common defects of a democratic society are shown in this extract upon the league?

When the next winter came Philip, having departed to Macedonia, and the Achaean Strategus, Eperatus, having incurred the contempt of the Achaean soldiers and the complete disregard of the mercenaries, no one would obey his orders, and no preparation was made for the defense of the country. This was observed by Pyrrhias, who had been sent by the Aetolians to command the Eleans. . . . He now began committing frequent raids, not only upon the territories of Dyme and Pharae, but upon that of Patrae also. . . . The result was that the cities, being exposed to much suffering, and unable to obtain any assistance, began to make difficulties about paying their contribution to the league; and the soldiers, finding their pay always in arrear and never paid at the right time, acted in the same way about going to the relief of the towns. Both parties, thus mutually retaliating on each other, affairs went from bad to worse, and at last the foreign contingent broke up altogether. And all this was the result of the incompetence of the chief magistrate. The time for the next election finding the Achaean affairs in this state, Eperatus laid down his office, and just at the beginning of summer Aratus the elder was elected Strategus. (V, 30.)

Now, when Aratus came into office he found the

mercenary army of the league in a state of complete demoralization, and the cities very slack to pay the tax for their support, owing to the bad and spiritless manner in which his predecesssor, Eperatus, had managed the affairs of the league. He, however, exhorted the members of the league to reform, and obtained a decree dealing with this matter; and then threw himself with energy into the preparation for the war. The decree passed by the Achaeans ordered the maintenance of eight thousand mecenary infantry and five hundred horse, together with three thousand Achaean infantry and three hundred horse, enrolled in the usual way; and that of these latter five hundred foot and fifty horse were to be brazen-shield men from Megalopolis, and the same number of Argives. It ordered also that three ships should be manned to cruise off Acte and in the Argolic gulf, and three off Patrae and Dyme, and in the sea there. (V, 91.)

QUESTIONS.

1. Enumerate the ills from which the league suffered under Eperatus. 2. How did the situation change under Aratus? 3. To what was the change due? 4. Did the Strategus generally lay down his office before his successor had been elected? 5. Make an outline and write a paper upon the Achaean league, citing evidence.

THE ROMAN CONSTITUTION.

CHAPTER VI.

THE ROMAN CONSTITUTION.

The Histories of Polybius. Translated from the text of F. Hultsch by Evelyn S. Schuckburgh, M. A. 2 vols. New York, 1889.

A BRIEF sketch of the life of Polybius was given in the preceding chapter of the STUDIES, and it is unnecessary to repeat it here. Emphasis should, however, be laid upon three points, two of which have been mentioned before, namely, the training of Polybius as a statesman, his excellent opportunity to study the Roman constitution through his sixteen years of residence in Rome, and the great importance that he himself attached to this institution.

The value of the observations of a witness depends largely upon his powers of observation. "The eye sees in an object what the eye brings power of seeing." Now, Polybius had a well-trained eye. He was familiar with all the constitutions of Greece and knew their merits and defects. The portions of his work in which he compares the constitutions of Sparta and Athens with the constitution of Rome are among the most valuable things that he wrote. In speaking of the Athenian constitution he affirmed that "its highest perfection was attained during the brilliant career of Themistocles; and having reached that point it quickly declined, owing to its essential instability. For the Athenian demus is always in the position of a ship without a commander. In such a ship, if fear of the enemy or the occurrence of a storm induce the crew to be of one mind and to obey the helmsman, everything goes well, but if they recover from this fear and begin to treat their officers with contempt and to quarrel with each other because they are no longer all of one mind,—one party wishing to continue the voyage and the other urging the steersman to bring the ship to anchor; some letting out the sheets and others hauling them in and ordering the sails to be furled,—then discords and quarrels make a sorry show to lookers on." (VI, 44.)

Of the Spartan constitution he said "that for guarding their own country with absolute safety and for preserving their own freedom the legislation of Lycurgus was entirely sufficient; and for those who are content with these objects we must concede that there neither exists, nor ever has existed, a constitution and civil order superior to that of Sparta." (VI, 50.)

But "if any one is seeking aggrandisement . . . the Spartan constitution is deficient, and that of Rome superior and better constituted for obtaining power." (VI, 50.)

Besides holding office in the Achaean league, Polybius was constantly engaged in diplomatic affairs during the larger part of his political life. This training made him a witness perfectly capable of dealing with such questions as the constitution of a state; he could treat such matters as a specialist.

But it is not only necessary that a witness should be capable of observation; he should also have sufficient opportunity to observe. Here again Polybius meets the requirements. He had studied the Roman constitution under many different aspects. In Rome itself he had followed its workings year after year, and had been aided in his efforts to understand it by some of the greatest of the Romans, men who were his daily companions. He had seen the Roman citizen as a soldier and had been present at the fall of Carthage; while in the organization of new territory that had fallen to Rome in Greece he had himself been a prominent factor.

But he was a Greek and looked upon the Roman institutions with the keen eyes of a countryman of Aristotle and of one who understood their tremendous importance. He appreciated the significance of the great empire that Rome had built up and he wrote his history that others might appreciate it too. Among the causes that contributed to make Rome mistress of the Mediterranean he counts the Roman constitution of primary importance.

TRIPLE ELEMENT IN THE ROMAN CONSTITUTION.

As for the Roman constitution, it had three elements, each of them possessing sovereign powers: and their respective share of power in the whole state had been regulated with such a scrupulous regard to equality and equilibrium that no one could say for certain, not even a native, whether the constitution as a whole were an aristocracy or a democracy or despotism. And no wonder: for if we confine our observation to the power of the Consuls we should be inclined to regard it as despotic; if on that of the Senate, as aristocratic; and if finally one look at the power possessed by the people it would seem a clear case of democracy. What the exact powers of these several parts were, and still, with slight modifications, are, I will now state. (VI, 11.)

QUESTIONS.

1. Define the terms "aristocracy," "democracy," "despotism." 2. Why did Polybius find difficulty in classifying the Roman constitution? 3. How could each of the elements possess "sovereign powers" and equality and equilibrium be maintained in the state? 4. Was Polybius describing the constitution of his own day?

THE CONSULS.

The Consuls, before leading out the legions, remain in Rome and are supreme masters of the administration. All other magistrates, except the Tribunes, are under them and take their orders. They introduce foreign ambassadors to the Senate; bring matters requiring deliberation before it; and see to the execution of its decrees. If, again, there are any matters of state which require the authorization of the people, it is their business to see to them, to summon the popular meetings, to bring the proposals before them and to carry out the decrees of the majority. In the preparations for war, also, and, in a word, in the entire administration of a campaign, they have all but absolute power. It is competent to them to impose on the allies such levies as they think good, to appoint the Military Tribunes, to make up the roll for soldiers, and to select those that are suitable. Besides, they have absolute power of afflicting punishment on all who are under their command while on active service; and they have authority to expend as much of the public money as they choose, being accompanied by a Quaestor, who is entirely at their orders. A survey of these powers would, in fact, justify our describing the constitution as despotic,—a clear case of royal government. Nor will it affect the truth of my description, if any of the institutions I have described are changed in our time, or in that of our posterity; and the same remarks apply to what follows. (VI, 12.)

QUESTIONS.

1. Make a list of the powers possessed by the Consuls, classifying them under such heads as War, Law, Administration, etc. 2. Enumerate the checks upon the Consul's power and show how important they were. 3. What would we call the Quaestor to-day? 4. Why was the Consul allowed to spend as much of the public money as he chose? 5. Compare the powers of the Consuls with those of our President. 6. Why has this change taken place in our day?

THE SENATE.

The Senate has first of all the control of the treasury, and regulates the receipts and disbursements alike. For the Quaestors cannot isssue any public money for the various departments of the state without a decree of the Senate, except for the service of the Consuls. The Senate controls also what is by far the largest and most important expenditure, that, namely, which is made by the censors every lustrum (five years) for the repair or construction of public buildings; this money cannot be obtained by the censors except by the grant of the Senate. Similarly all crimes committed in Italy requiring a public investigation, such as treason, conspiracy, poisoning, or wilful murder, are in the hands of the Senate. Besides, if any individual or state among the Italian allies requires a controversy to be settled, a penalty to be assessed, help of protection to be afforded,—all this is the province of the Senate. Or again, outside of Italy, if it is necessary to send an embassy to reconcile warring communities, or to remind them of their duty, or sometimes to impose requisitions upon them, or to receive their submission, or finally to proclaim war against them,— this too is the business of the Senate. With such business the people have nothing to do. Consequently, if one were staying at Rome when the Consuls were not in town, one would imagine the constitution to be a complete aristocracy: and this has been the idea entertained by many Greeks, and by many kings as well, from the fact that nearly all the business they had with Rome was settled by the Senate. (VI, 13.)

QUESTIONS.

1. Make a list of the powers of the Senate, classifying them. 2. What body or bodies in our government possess the powers held by the Roman Senate? 3. Which arrangement is better and why? 4. What men in our state government perform the duties here ascribed to the censors?

THE PEOPLE

After this one would naturally be inclined to ask what part is left for the people in the constitution, when the Senate has these various functions, especially the control of the receipts and expenditures of the exchequer; and when the Consuls, again, have absolute power over the details of military preparation, and an absolute authority in the field? There is, however, a part left the people, and it is a most important one. For the people is the sole fountain of honor and of punishment; and it is by these two things and these alone that dynasties and constitutions, and, in a word, human society are held together: for where the distinction between them is not sharply drawn, both in theory and practice, there no undertaking can be properly administered,—as indeed we might expect when good and bad are held in exactly the same honor. The people then are the only court to decide matters of life and death; and even in cases where the penalty is money, if the sum to be assessed is sufficiently serious, and especially when the accused have held the high magistracies. And in regard to this arrangement there is one point deserving especial commendation and record. Men who are on trial for their lives at Rome, while sentence is in process of being voted,—if even one of the tribes whose votes are needed to ratify the sentence has not voted,—have the privilege at Rome of openly departing and condemning themselves to a voluntary exile. Such men are safe at Naples or Praeneste or at Tibur, and at other towns with which this arrangement has been duly ratified on oath.

Again, it is the people who bestow offices on the deserving, which are the most honorable rewards of virtue. It has also the absolute power of passing and repealing laws; and most important of all, it is the people who deliberate on the question of peace or war. And when provisional terms are made for alliance, suspension of hostilities, or treaties, it is the people who ratify them or the reverse.

These considerations again would lead one to say that the chief power in the state was the people's, and that the constitution was a democracy. (VI, 14.)

QUESTIONS.

1. Enumerate the powers of the people and classify them. 2. Indicate the importance of each. 3. Who exercises these powers in our government? 4. Why must a man decide to go into exile before the *last* tribe has voted? 5. Why were not exiles safe elsewhere than at Naples, Praeneste, and Tibur?

MUTUAL RELATION OF THE THREE.—CONSUL DEPENDENT ON SENATE AND PEOPLE.

Such, then, is the distribution of power between the several parts of the state. I must now show how each of these several parts can, when they choose, oppose or support each other.

The Consul, then, when he has started on an expedition with the powers I have described, is to all appearance absolute in the administration of the business in hand; still he has need of the support both of people and of Senate, and without them is quite unable to bring the matter to a successful conclusion. For it is plain that he must have supplies sent to his legions from time to time; but without a decree of the Senate they can be supplied neither with corn, nor clothes, nor pay, so that all the plans of a commander must be futile if the Senate is resolved either to shrink from danger or hamper his plans. And again, whether a Consul shall bring any undertaking to a conclusion or no depends entirely upon the Senate: for it has absolute authority at the end of a year to send another Consul to supersede him, or to continue the existing one in his command. Again, even to the successes of the generals, the Senate has the power to add distinction and glory, and on the other hand to obscure their merits and lower their credit. For these high achievements are brought in tangible form before the eyes of the citizens by what are called "triumphs." But these triumphs the commanders cannot celebrate with proper pomp, or in some cases celebrate at all, unless the Senate concurs and grants the necessary money. As for the people, the Consuls are pre-eminently obliged to court their favor, however distant from home may be the field of their operations; for it is the people, as I have said before, that ratifies, or refuses to ratify, terms of peace and treaties; but most of all because when laying down their office they have to give an account of their administration before it. Therefore in no case is it safe for the Consuls to neglect either the Senate or the good will of the people. (VI, 15.)

QUESTIONS.

1. Where is the power of the Consuls practically absolute? 2. When did the Senate have the greatest opportunity to increase its power? 3. How do you reconcile the statement above about the dependence of the Consul upon the Senate with the statement in a previous extract that the money for the service of the Consuls was issued without a decree of the Senate? 4. Show all the ways in which the Senate might ill-treat a Consul whom it disliked.

THE SENATE CONTROLLED BY THE PEOPLE.

As to the Senate, which possess the immense power I have described, in the first place it is obliged, in public affairs, to take the multitude into account, and respect the wishes of the people; and it cannot put into execution the penalty for offences against the republic which are punishable by death, unless the people first ratify its decrees. Similarly, even in matters which directly affect the senators—for instance, in the case of a law diminishing the Senate's traditional authority, or depriving senators of certain dignities and offices, or even actually cutting down their property,—even in such cases the people have the sole power of passing or rejecting the law. But most important of all is the fact that, if the Tribunes interpose their veto, the Senate not only are unable to pass a decree, but cannot even hold a meeting at all, whether formal or informal. Now, the Tribunes are always bound to carry out the decree of the people, and above all things to have regard to their wishes: therefore, for all these reasons the Senate stands in awe of the multitude, and cannot neglect the feelings of the people. (VI, 16.)

QUESTIONS.

1. Under what circumstances is the power of the people greater than that of the Senate? 2. What is the great advantage that the Senate has? 3. What is its most dangerous opponent and why? 4. Why would the Senate be naturally conservative?

THE PEOPLE DEPENDENT ON THE SENATE AND CONSUL.

In like manner the people on its part is far from being independent of the Senate, and is bound to take its wishes into account, both collectively and individually. For contracts, too numerous to count, are given out by the censors in all parts of Italy for the repairs or construction of public buildings; there is also the collection of revenue from many rivers, harbors, gardens, mines, and land,—everything, in a word, that comes under the control of the Roman government: and in all these the people at large are engaged; so that there is scarcely a man, so to speak, who is not interested either as a contractor or as being employed in the works. For some purchase the contracts from the censors themselves; and others go partners with them; while others again go security for these contractors, or actually pledge their property to the treasury for them. Now over all these transactions the Senate has absolute control. It can grant an extension of time; and in case of unforeseen accident can relieve the contractors from a portion of their obligation, or release them from it altogether, if they are absolutely unable to fulfill it. And there are many details in which the Senate can inflict great hardships, or, on the other hand, grant great indulgences to the contractors; for in every case the appeal is to it. But the most important point of all is that the judges are taken from its members in the majority of trials, whether public or private, in which the charges are heavy. Consequently all citizens are much at its mercy; and being alarmed at the uncertainty as to when they may need its aid, are cautious about resisting or actively opposing its will. And for a similar reason men do not rashly resist the wishes of the Consuls, because one and all may become subject to their absolute authority on a campaign. (VI, 17.)

QUESTIONS.

1. What ties bind the people to Senate and Consuls? 2. What condition of things in our government is similar to the relation of the people to the Senate? 3. Was the feeling that prompted obedience to the Consuls an ideal one? 4. How might the Consuls abuse this advantage?

A FIRM UNION FOR ALL EMERGENCIES.

The result of this power of the several estates for mutual help or harm is a union sufficiently firm for all emergencies, and a constitution than which it is impossible to find a better. For whenever any danger from without compels them to unite and work together, the strength which is developed by the state is so extraordinary that everything required is unfailingly carried out by the eager rivalry shown by all classes to devote their whole minds to the need of the hour, and to secure that any determination come to should not fail for want of promptitude; while each individual works, privately and publicly alike, for the accomplishment of the business in hand. Accordingly the peculiar constitution of the state makes it irresistible, and certain of obtaining whatever it determines to attempt. Nay, even when these external alarms are past, and the people are enjoying their good fortune and the fruits of their victories, and, as usually happens, growing corrupted by flattery and idleness, show a tendency to violence and arrogance,—it is in these circumstances, more than ever, that the constitution is seen to possess within itself the power of correcting abuses. For when any one of the three classes becomes puffed up and manifests an inclination to be contentious and unduly encroaching, the mutual interdependency of all the three, and the possibility of the pretensions of any one being checked and thwarted by the others, must plainly check this tendency: and so the proper equilibrium is maintained by the impulsiveness of the one part being checked by its fear of the other. . . . . (VI, 18.)

QUESTIONS.

1. What was evidently the one condition upon which the successful working of the constitution depended? 2. Explain, making use of the above extracts, how the encroachments of one element in the constitution might be checked by the others. 3. What are the defects of the Roman constitution? 4. Make a table of the Roman constitution, showing how power was divided, making use of all the material supplied in the above extracts.

ON THE ROMAN ARMY.

After electing Consuls they proceed to elect military tribunes,—fourteen from those who had five years', and ten from those who had ten years', service. All citizens must serve ten years in the cavalry or twenty years in the infantry before the forty-sixth year of their age, except those rated below four hundred asses. The latter are employed in the navy; but if any great public necessity arises they are obliged to serve as infantry also for twenty campaigns; and no one can hold an office in the state until he has completed ten years of military service. . . .

THE LEVY.

When the Consuls are about to enroll the army they give public notice of the day on which all Roman citizens of military age must appear. This is done every year. When the day has arrived, and the citizens fit for service have come to Rome and have assembled on the Capitoline, the fourteen junior tribunes divide themselves, in the order in which they were appointed by the people or by the Imperators, into four divisions, because the primary division of the forces thus raised is into four legions. The four tribunes first appointed are assigned to the legion called the 1st; the next three to the 2d; the next four to the 3d; and the three last to the 4th. Of the ten senior tribunes, the two first are assigned to the 1st legion; the next three to the 2d; the two next to the 3d; and the three last to the 4th. (VI, 19.)

QUESTIONS.

1. What was the principal way in which a Roman served the state? 2. How were Consuls and Tribunes chosen? 3. How were young men practically excluded from holding office in the state? 4. What were the three branches of service and their relative importance? 5. Why were the Tribunes distributed in this peculiar manner among the legions?

THE DISTRIBUTION OF RECRUITS.

This division and assignment of the tribunes having been settled in such a way that all four legions have an equal number of officers, the Tribunes of the several legions take up a separate position and draw lots for the tribes, one by one; and summon the tribe on whom it from time to time falls. From this tribe they select four young men as nearly like each other in age and physical strength as possible. These four are brought forward, and the Tribunes of the first legion pick out one of them, those of the second another, those of the third another, and the fourth has to take the last. When the next four are selected the Tribunes of the second legion have the first choice, and those of the first the last. With the next four the Tribunes of the third legion have the first choice, those of the second the last; and so on in regular rotation: of which the result is that each legion gets men of much the same standard. But when they have selected the number prescribed,—which is four thousand two hundred infantry for each legion, or at times of special danger five thousand,—they next used to pass men for the cavalry, in old times after the four thousand two hundred infantry; but now they do it before them, the selection having been made by the censor on the basis of wealth; and they enroll three hundred for each legion. (VI, 20.)

QUESTIONS.

1. Give the probable reasons for the different steps taken in enrolling men. 2. What difference existed between the manner of choosing men for the infantry and for the cavalry?

TAKING THE OATH.

The roll having been completed in this manner, the Tribunes belonging to the several legions muster their men; and selecting one of the whole body that they think most suitable for the purpose, they cause him to take an oath that he will obey his officers and do their orders to the best of his ability. And all the others come up and take the oath separately, merely affirming that they will do the same as the first man.

At the same time the Consuls send orders to the magistrates of the allied cities in Italy, from which they determine that allied troops are to serve: declaring the number required, and the day and place at which the men selected must appear. The cities then enroll their troops with much the same ceremonies as to selection and administration of the oath, and appoint a commander and a paymaster.

FOURFOLD DIVISION OF THE LEGIONARIES.

The military Tribunes at Rome, after the administering of the oath to their men, and giving out the day and place at which they are to appear without arms, for the present dismiss them. When they arrive on the appointed day, they first select the youngest and poorest to form the Velites, the next to them the Hastati, while those who are in the prime of life they select as Principes, and the oldest of all the Triarii. For in the Roman army these divisions, distinct not only as to their ages and nomenclature, but also as to the manner in which they are armed, exist in each legion. The division is made in such proportions that the senior men, called Triarii, should number six hundred, the Principes twelve hundred, the Hastati twelve hundred, and that all the rest as the youngest should be reckoned among the Velites. And if the whole number of the legion is more than four thousand, they vary the numbers of these divisions proportionally, except those of the Triarii, which is always the same. (VI, 21.)

QUESTIONS.

1. Why was not the oath administered in the same way to all the men? 2. What relations existed between the Consuls and the allied troops? 3. What was the probable object in dividing the Roman soldiers into Velites, Hastati, Principes, and Triarii?

ELECTION OF CENTURIONS.

The Principes, Hastati, and Triarii, each elect ten centurions according to merit, and then a second ten each. All these sixty have the title of centurion alike, of whom the first man chosen is a member of the council of war. And they in their turn select a rear-rank officer who is called optio. Next in conjunction with the centurions they divide the several orders (omitting the Velites) into ten companies each, and appoint to each company two centurions and two optiones; the Velites are divided equally among all the companies; these companies are called orders (ordines) or maniples (manipuli), or vexilla, and their officers are called centurions or ordinum ductores. Each maniple selects two of their strongest and best born men as standard bearers (vexillarii). And that each maniple should have two commanding officers is only reasonable; for it being impossible to know what a commander may be doing or what may happen to him, and necessities of war admitting of no parleying, they are anxious that the maniple may never be without a leader and commander. When the two centurions are both on the field, the first elected commands the right of the maniple, the second the left: if both are not there, the one who is commands the whole. And they wish the centurions not to be so much bold and adventurous, as men with a faculty for command, steady, and of a profound rather than of a showy spirit; not prone to engage wantonly or be unnecessarily forward in giving battle; but such as in the face of superior numbers and overwhelming pressure will die in defense of their post. (VI, 24.)

QUESTIONS.

Make a diagram showing the men and officers composing a legion, giving the name of each.

OFFICERS AND ARMS OF THE EQUITES.

Similarly they divide the cavalry into ten squadrons (turmae), and from each they select three officers (decuriones), who each select a subaltern (optio). The decurio first elected commands the squadron, the other two have the rank of decuriones: a name, indeed, which applies to all alike. If the first decurio is not on the field, the second takes command of the squadron. The armor of the cavalry is very like that in Greece. In old times they did not wear the lorica, but fought in their tunics (campestria); the result of which was that they were prompt and nimble at dismounting and mounting again with dispatch, but were in great danger at close quarters from the unprotected state of their bodies. And their lances, too, were useless in two ways: first, because they were thin and prevented their taking a good aim; and before they could get the head fixed in the enemy the lances were so shaken by the mere motion of the horse that they generally broke. Secondly, because having no spike at the butt end of their lance, they only had one stroke, namely, that with the spear head; and if the lance broke, what was left in their hands was entirely useless. Again, they used to have shields of bull's hide, just like those round cakes, with a knob in the middle, which are used at sacrifices, which were useless at close quarters because they were flexible rather than firm; and when their leather shrunk and rotted from the rain, unserviceable as they were before, they then became entirely so. Wherefore, as experience showed them the uselessness of these, they lost no time in changing to the Greek fashion of arms: the advantages of which were, first, that men were able to deliver the first stroke of their lance-head with a good aim and effect, and because the shaft from the nature of its construction was steady and not quivering; and secondly, they were able by reversing the lance, to use the spike at the butt end for a steady and effective blow. And the same may be said about the Greek shields: for whether used to ward off a blow or to thrust against the enemy, they neither give nor bend. When the Romans learnt these facts about the Greek arms they were not long in copying them; for no nation has ever surpassed them in readiness to adopt new fashions from other people, and to imitate what they see is better in others than themselves. (VI, 25.)

QUESTIONS.

1. What one great cause of Roman success is indicated by Polybius in this extract? 2. Draw a diagram of a squadron of cavalry. 3. What changes had been made in the equipment of the cavalry in Polybius' day and why?

ASSEMBLY OF LEGIONS—THE SOCII (ALLIES).

Having made this distribution of their men and given orders for their being armed, as I have described, the military tribunes dismiss them to their homes. But when the day has arrived on which they were all bound by their oath to appear at the place named by the Consuls (for each Consul generally appoints a separate place for his own legions, each having assigned to him two legions and a moiety of the allies), all whose names appear on the roll appear without fail: no excuse being accepted in case of those who have accepted the oath, except a prohibitory omen of absolute impossibility. The allies muster along with the citizens, and are distributed and managed by the officers appointed by the Consuls, who have the title of Praefecti sociis and are twelve in number. These officers select for the Consuls from the whole infantry and cavalry of the allies such as are most fitted for actual service, and these are called extraordinarii. . . . . . . The whole number of the infantry of the socii generally equals that of the legions, but the cavalry is treble that of the citizens. Of these they select a third of the cavalry and a fifth of the infantry to serve as extraordinarii. The rest they divide into two parts, one of which is called the right, the other the left wing (alae). (VI, 26.)

QUESTIONS.

Make a table showing the officers of the Roman army in order of rank, how they secure office, and conditions (when given). Enumerate all the different bodies of troops with their subdivisions and the number of men in each.

ROMAN LIFE OF THE FIRST PUNIC WAR.

CHAPTER VII.

ROMAN LIFE OF THE FIRST PUNIC WAR.

The Histories of Polybius. Translated from the text of F. Hultsch by Evelyn S. Schuckburgh, M. A. 2 vols. New York, 1889.

IN the preceding chapter, extracts were given from Polybius upon the Roman constitution at the time of its greatest effectiveness. In this chapter, it is my purpose to show, by extracts from the same writer, what the character of the Roman people was, and how the constitution stood the test of a great foreign war in which Rome was matched against a foeman worthy of her steel. Polybius says of this period that the Roman "institutions were as yet in their original integrity," and if one would obtain "a fair view of the national characteristics," one should examine them at this time.

It is my intention, in the following chapters of the Studies, to treat of life under the decaying republic, as shown by Sallust, Cicero, and others; to draw a picture of life under the empire from the letters of Pliny, and to conclude with extracts from the institutes of Justinian, illustrative of Roman law, that most typical product of Roman civilization. In the fifth and sixth chapters of the Studies, something has been said about the life of Polybius, and the value of the evidence that he offers us. It remains to add a word upon the value of the extracts employed in this study.

Polybius was not a contemporary of the First

Punic War, but he was able to converse with the sons of the men who fought in the war and might even have spoken with some of the survivors of that generation. We know that he had before him contemporary accounts of the war written by Romans and Carthaginians. He refers to the work of the Carthaginian Philinus and the Roman Fabius, "who bore the reputation of writing with the most complete knowledge about it (the war)" but adds that they have "given us an inadequate representation of the truth." (I, 14.) He certainly had other sources of information, for when these two writers make statements that "nothing can reconcile," he is able to control them.

THE BEGINNING OF THE WAR.

Thus were the Mamertines first deprived of support from Rhegium, and then subjected, from causes which I have just stated, to a complete defeat on their own account. Thereupon some of them betook themselves to the protection of the Carthaginians, and were for putting themselves and their citadel into their hands; while others set about sending an embassy to Rome to offer a surrender of their city and to beg assistance on the ground of the ties of race which united them. The Romans were long in doubt. The inconsistency of sending such aid seemed manifest. A little while ago they had put some of their own citizens to death, with the extreme penalties of the law, for having broken faith with the people of Rhegium; and now so soon afterwards to assist the Mamertines, who had done precisely the same to Messene as well as Rhegium, involved a breach of equity very hard to justify. But while fully alive to these points, they yet saw that Carthaginian aggrandisement was not confined to Lybia, but had embraced many districts in Iberia as well; and that Carthage was, besides, mistress of all the islands in the Sardinian and Tyrrhenian seas; they were beginning, therefore, to be exceedingly anxious lest, if the Carthaginians became masters of Sicily also, they should find them very dangerous and formidable neighbors, surrounding them as they would on every side, and occupying a position which commanded all the coasts of Italy. Now it was clear that, if the Mamertines did not obtain the assistance they asked for, the Carthaginians would very soon reduce Sicily. For should they avail themselves of the voluntary offer of Messene and become masters of it, they were certain before long to crush Syracuse also, since they were already lords of nearly the whole of the rest of Sicily. The Romans saw all this, and felt that it was absolutely necessary not to let Messene slip, or allow the Carthaginians to secure what would be like a bridge to enable them to cross into Italy. (I, 10.)

In spite of protracted deliberations, the conflict of motives proved too strong, after all, to allow of the Senate coming to any decision; for the inconsistency of aiding the Messenians appeared to them to be evenly balanced by the advantages to be gained by doing so. The people, however, had suffered much from the previous wars, and wanted some means of repairing the losses which they had sustained in every department. Besides these national advantages to be gained by the war, the military commanders suggested that individually they would get manifest and important benefits from it. They accordingly voted in favor of giving aid.
. . . The Roman Consul, Appius, for his part, gallantly crossed the strait by night and got into Messene. But he found that the enemy had completely surrounded the town and were vigorously pressing on the attack; and he concluded on reflection that the seige could bring him neither credit nor security so long as the enemy commanded land as well as sea. He accordingly first endeavored to relieve the Mamertines from the contest altogether by sending embassies to both of the attacking forces. Neither of them received the proposals, and at last, from sheer necessity, he made up his mind to hazard an engagement, and that he would begin with the Syracusans. So he led out his forces and drew them up for the fight; nor was the Syracusan backward in accepting the challenge, but descended simultaneously to give him battle. After a prolonged struggle, Appius got the better of the enemy and chased the opposing forces right up to their entrenchments. The result of this was that Appius, after stripping the dead, retired into Messene again, while Hiero, with a foreboding of the final result, only waited

for night-fall to beat a hasty retreat to Syracuse. (I, 11.)

Next morning, when Appius was assured of their flight, his confidence was strengthened, and he made up his mind to attack the Carthaginians without delay. Accordingly he issued orders to the soldiers to dispatch their preparations early, and at daybreak commenced his sally. Having succeeded in engaging the enemy, he killed a large number of them, and forced the rest to fly precipitately to the neighboring towns. These successes sufficed to raise the seige of Messene; and thenceforth he scoured the territory of the Syracusans and their allies with impunity and laid it waste without finding anyone to dispute the possession of the open country with him; and finally he sat down before Syracuse itself and laid seige to it. (I, 12.)

QUESTIONS.

1. Did the Romans attach much importance to good faith in dealing with other states? 2. What do you think of their reasons for action in this case? 3. Enumerate the lower motives that caused them to act. 4. Enumerate all the excellent traits of character brought out in this first struggle and indicate the value of each.

SIEGE OF AGRIGENTUM.

I shall, however, endeavor to describe with somewhat more care the first war which arose between the Romans and the Carthaginians for the possession of Sicily. For it would not be easy to mention any war that lasted longer than this one; nor one in which the preparations made were on a larger scale, or the efforts made more sustained, or the actual engagements more numerous, or the reverses sustained on either side more signal. Moreover, the two states themselves were at the precise period of their history when their institutions were as yet in their original integrity, their fortunes still at a moderate level, and their forces on an equal footing, so that those who wish to gain a fair view of the national characteristics and resources of the two had better base their comparison upon this war rather than upon those which came after. (I, 13.)

On the Roman side a change of commanders had now taken place. The consuls who made the treaty with Hiero had gone home, and their successors, Lucius

Postumius and Quintus Mamilius, were come to Sicily with their legions. Observing the measures which the Carthaginians were taking, and the forces they were concentrating at Agrigentum, they made up their minds to take that matter in hand and strike a bold blow. Accordingly they suspended every other department of the war, and bearing down upon Agrigentum with their whole army attacked it in force; pitched their camp within a distance of eight stades from the city; and confined the Carthaginians within the walls. Now it was just harvest time, and the siege was evidently destined to be a long one; the soldiers, therefore, went out to collect the corn with greater hardihood than they ought to have done. Accordingly the Carthaginians, seeing the enemy scattered about the fields, sallied out and attacked the harvesting party. They easily routed these; and then one portion of them made a rush to destroy the Roman intrenchment, the other to attack the pickets. But the peculiarity of their institutions saved the Roman fortunes, as it had often done before. Among them it is death for a man to desert his post, or to fly from his station on any pretext whatever. Accordingly on this, as on other occasions, they gallantly held their ground against opponents many times their own number; and though they lost many of their own men, they killed still more of the enemy and at last outflanked the foes just as they were on the point of demolishing the palisade of the camp. Some they put to the sword, and the rest they pursued with slaughter into the city. (I, 17.)

QUESTIONS.

1. What should you infer, from the first paragraph, as to comparative strength of Rome and Carthage? Why? 2. What bad practice of the Romans, from a military point of view, is mentioned in the second paragraph? 3. What do you think of the Roman plan of concentrating on Agrigentum? 4. What defects did the Romans show at this time? 5. What good qualities? 6. What proof of Roman organization and discipline do you find?

THE CREATION OF A NAVY.

Great was the joy of the Roman Senate when the news of what had taken place at Agrigentum arrived, their ideas, too, were so raised that they no longer confined themselves to their original designs. They were not content with having saved the Mamertines, nor with the advantages gained in the course of the war; but conceived the idea that it was possible to expel the Carthaginians entirely from the island, and that if that were done their own power would receive a great increase; they accordingly engaged in this policy and directed their whole thought to this subject. . . . Yet so long as the Carthaginians were in undisturbed command of the sea, the balance of success could not incline decisively in their favor. . . . They became eager to get upon the sea and meet the Carthaginians there.

It was this branch of the subject that more than anything else induced me to give an account of this war at somewhat greater length than I otherwise should have done. I was unwilling that a first step of this kind should be unknown,—namely, how, and when, and why the Romans first started a navy.

It was, then, because they saw that the war they had undertaken lingered to a weary length, that they first thought of getting a fleet built, consisting of a hundred quinqueremes and twenty triremes. But one part of their undertaking caused them much difficulty. Their ship builders were entirely unacquainted with the construction of quinqueremes, because no one in Italy had at that time employed vessels of that description. There could be no more signal proof of the courage, or rather the extraordinary audacity of the Roman enterprise. Not only had they no resources for it of reasonable sufficiency; but without any resources for it at all, and without having ever entertained an idea of naval war,—for it was the first time they had thought of it,—they nevertheless handled the enterprise with such extraordinary audacity that, without so much as a preliminary trial, they took upon themselves there and then to meet the Carthaginians at sea, on which they had for generations held undisputed supremacy. Proof of what I say, and of their surprising audacity may be found in this: When they first took in hand to send troops across to Messene, they not only had no decked vessels, but no war ships at all, not so much as a single galley; but they borrowed quinqueremes and triremes from Tarentum and Locri, and even from Elea and Neapolis; and having thus collected a fleet boldly sent their men across upon it. It was on this occasion that, the Carthaginians having put to sea in the strait to attack them, a decked vessel of theirs charged so furiously that it ran aground, and falling into the hands of the Romans served them as a model on which they constructed their whole fleet. And if this had not happened, it is clear that they would have been completely hindered from carrying out their designs by want of constructive knowledge. (I,20.)

Meanwhile, however, those who were charged with the shipbuilding were busy with the construction of the vessels; while others collected crews and were engaged in teaching them to row on dry land; which they contrived to do in the following manner. They made men sit on rowers' benches on dry land, in the same order as they would sit on the benches in actual vessels. In the midst of them they stationed the celeustes and trained them to get back and draw in their hands altogether in time, and then to swing forward and throw them out again, and to begin and cease these movements at the word of the celeustes. By the time these preparations were completed the ships were built. They therefore launched them, and, after a brief preliminary practice of real sea rowing, started on their coasting voyage along the shore of Italy in accordance with the Consul's order. (I, 21.)

QUESTIONS.

1. What was the danger in the new designs of the Romans? 2. Why should Polybius consider the building of a navy such an important matter. 3. Enumerate all the admirable characteristics brought out in the above passage.

ROMAN INGENUITY.

When the Romans had neared the coast of Sicily and had learnt the disaster which had b fa len Gnaeus, their first step was to send for Gaius Duilius, who was in command of the land forces. Until he should come they stayed where they were; but at the same time, hearing that the enemy's fleet was no great way off, they busied themselves in preparation for a sea-fight. Now the ships were badly fitted out and not easy to manage, and so some one suggested to them as likely to serve their turn in the fight the construction of what were afterwards called "crows." Their mechanism was this. A round pole was placed in the prow about twenty-four feet high, and with a diameter of four palms. The pole itself had a pulley on the top and a gangway made with cross planks nailed together, four feet wide and thirty-six feet long, was made to swing round it. Now the hole in the gangway was oval shape, and went round the pole twelve feet from one end of the gangway, which had also a wooden railing running down each side of it to the height of a man's knee. At the extremity of this gangway was fastened an iron spike like a miller's pestle, sharpened at its lower end, and fitted with a ring at its upper end. The whole thing looked like the machines for braising corn. To this ring the rope was fastened with which, when the ships collided, they hauled up the "crows" by means of the pulley at the top of the pole, and dropped them down upon the deck of the enemy's ship, sometimes over the prow, sometimes swinging them round when the ships collided broadsides. And as soon as the "crows" were fixed in the planks of the decks and grappled the ships together, if the ships were along side of each other, the men leaped on board anywhere along the side, but if they were prow to prow, they used the "crow" itself for boarding, and advanced over it two abreast. The first two protected their front by holding up before them their shields, while those who came after them secured their sides by placing the rims of their shields upon the top of the rails. Such were the preparations which they made; and having completed them they watched an opportunity of engaging at sea. (I, 22.)

QUESTIONS.

1. Why did the Romans wish to grapple with the Carthaginians? 2. What effect did the use of "crows" have upon a naval battle?

THE INVASION OF AFRICA.

Now it was the purpose of the Romans to sail across to Lybia and transfer the war there, in order that the Carthaginians might find the danger affecting themselves and their own country rather than Sicily. But the Carthaginians were determined to prevent this. They knew that Lybia was easily invaded, and that the invaders, if they once effected a landing, would meet with little resistance from the inhabitants; and they therefore made up their minds not to allow it, and were eager rather to bring the matter to a decisive issue by a battle at sea. The one side was determined to cross, the other to prevent their crossing; and their enthusiastic rivalry gave promise of a desperate struggle. The preparations of the Romans were made to suit either contingency, an engagement at sea or a disembarkation on the enemy's soil. Accordingly they picked out the best hands from the land army and divided the whole force which they meant to take on board into four divisions. (I, 26.)

QUESTIONS.

1. What do you think of the Romans' plan of invading Africa? 2. Was it in keeping with their character? 3. What Roman characteristic is brought out in the account of the preparations?

SIEGE OF ASPIS.

After the battle the Romans took in a fresh supply of victuals, repaired and refitted the ships they had captured, bestowed upon the crews the attention which they had deserved by their victory, and then put to sea with a view of continuing their voyage to Lybia. The leading ships made the shore just under the headland called the Hermaeum, which is the extreme point on the east of the Gulf of Carthage and runs out into the open sea in the direction of Sicily. There they waited for the rest of the ships to come up, and having got the entire fleet together, coasted along until they came to the city called Aspis. Here they disembarked, beached their ships, dug a trench, and constructed a stockade around them; and on the inhabitants of the city refusing to submit without compulsion, they set to work to besiege the town. Presently those of the Carthaginians who had survived the sea fight came to land also; and feeling sure that the enemy, in the flush of their victory, intended to sail straight against Carthage itself, they began by keeping a chain of advanced guards at outlying points to protect the capital with their military and naval forces. But when they ascertained that the Romans had disembarked without resistance and were engaged in besieging Aspis, they gave up the idea of watching for the descent of the fleet, but concentrated their forces and devoted themselves to the protection of the capital and its environs. (I, 29.)

QUESTIONS.

1. What action performed by the Romans after landing illustrates one side of their character? 2. Why would it not have been wiser to attack Carthage at once?

REGULUS DICTATES TO THE CARTHAGINIANS.

But Regulus had different views. The double defeat sustained by the Carthaginians, by land as well as by sea, convinced him that the capture of Carthage was a question of a very short time, and he was in a state of great anxiety lest his successor in the consulship should arrive from Rome in time to rob him of the glory of the achievement. He therefore invited the Carthaginians to make terms. They were only too glad of the proposal, and sent their leading citizens to meet him. The meeting took place, but the commissioners could not bring their minds to entertain his proposals; they were so severe that it was almost more than they could bear to listen to them at all. Regulus regarded himself as practically master of the city, and considered that they ought to regard any concession on his part as a matter of favor and pure grace. The Carthaginians, on the other hand, concluded that nothing worse could be imposed on them if they suffered capture than was now enjoined. They therefore returned home without accepting the offers of Regulus, and extremely exasperated by his unreasonable harshness. (I, 31.)

QUESTIONS.

1. What unwise provision in the constitution is mentioned here? 2. Why was it unwise? 3. What defects in Regulus' character? 4. Have you met them before in these extracts? 5. Are they characteristic Roman traits?

SOME TRAITS OF ROMAN CHARACTER.

The passage was effected in safety, and the coast of Camerena was reached; but there they experienced so terrible a storm and suffered so dreadfully as almost to beggar description. The disaster was indeed extreme; for out of their three hundred and sixty-four vessels eighty only remained. The rest were either swamped or driven by the surf upon the rocks and headland, where they went to pieces and filled all the seaboard with corpses and wreckage. No greater catastrophe is to be found in all history as befalling a fleet at one time. And for this fortune was not so much to blame as the commanders themselves. They had been warned again and again by the pilots not to steer along the southern coast of Sicily facing the Lybian sea, because it was exposed and yielded no safe anchorage. . . . Yet they attended to none of these warnings, but intoxicated by their recent success, were anxious to capture certain cities as they coasted along, and in pursuance of this idea thoughtlessly exposed themselves to the full fury of the open sea. As far as these particular men were concerned, the disaster which they brought upon themselves in pursuit of trivial advantages convinced them of the folly of their conduct. But it is a peculiarity of the Roman people as a whole to treat everything as a question of main strength; to consider that they must, of course, accomplish whatever they have proposed to themselves, and that nothing is impossible that they have once determined upon. The result of such self-confidence is that in many things they do succeed, while in some few they conspicuously fail, and especially at sea. On land it is against men only and their works that they have to direct their efforts, and as the forces against which they exert their strength do not differ intrinsically from their own, as a general rule they succeed; while their failures are exceptionally rare. But to contend with the sea and sky is to fight against a force immeasurably superior to their own; and when they trust to an exertion of sheer strength in such a contest the disasters which they meet with are signal. This is what they experienced on the present occasion; they have often experienced it since, and will continue to do so as long as they maintain their headstrong and foolhardy notions that any season of the year admits of sailing as well as marching. (I, 37.)

The Roman government, when they heard of this from the survivors of the wreck on their arrival home, felt it to be a grievous misfortune; but being absolutely resolved not to give in, they determined once more to put two hundred and fifty vessels on the stocks and build afresh. These were finished in three months, an almost incredibly short time, and the new consuls, Aulus Atilius and Gnaeus Cornelius, fitted out a fleet and put to sea. (I, 38.)

QUESTIONS.

1. Enumerate the Roman traits brought out in these passages, classifying under good and bad. 2. Show how the gain from the excellent traits more than overbalanced the loss from the bad traits.

SIEGE OF LILYBAEUM.

The Romans made two camps, one on each side of the town, and connected them with a ditch, stockade, and wall. Having done this, they began the assault by advancing their siege works in the direction of the tower nearest the sea, which commands a view of the Lybian main. They did this gradually, always adding something to what they had already constructed, and thus bit by bit pushed their works forward and extended them laterally, till at last they had brought down not only this tower, but the six next to it also, and at the same time began battering all the others with battering rams. The siege was carried on with vigor and terrific energy; every day some of the towers were shaken, and others reduced to ruins; every day, too, the siege works advanced farther and farther and more and more towards the heart of the city, and though there were in the town, besides the ordinary inhabitants, as many as ten thousand hired soldiers, the consternation and despondency became overwhelming. Yet their commander, Himilco, omitted no measure within his power. As fast as the enemy demolished a fortification he threw up a new one; he also countermined them, and reduced the assailants to straits of no ordinary difficulty. Moreover, he made daily sallies, attempted to carry or throw fire into the siege works, and with this end in view fought many desperate invasions by night as well as by day; so determined was the fighting in these struggles that sometimes the number of the dead was greater than it ordinarily is in a pitched battle. (I, 42.)

QUESTIONS.

1. Point out everything in the above passages that proves the skill of the Romans in military science. 2. What other characteristics did they display during the siege?

TREATMENT OF ROMAN OFFICERS.

The result of this sea fight gave Adherbal a high reputation at Carthage, for his success was looked upon as wholly due to himself and his own foresight and courage; while at Rome Publius fell into great disrepute and was loudly censured as having, during his administration, as far as a single man could, involved Rome in serious disasters. He was accordingly, some time afterwards, brought to trial, was heavily fined, and exposed to considerable danger. Not that the Romans gave way in consequence of these events. On the contrary they omitted nothing that was in their power to do, and continued resolute to prosecute the campaign. (I, 52.)

QUESTIONS.

1. What influence would the treatment of Publius be likely to have upon other officers? 2. What seems to have been the effect of disaster upon the Romans? Cite other cases in support of your answer. 3. What is the most valuable trait that you have met with yet?

MORE ROMAN CHARACTERISTICS—THE FINAL STRUGGLE.

The fact is that before either party had completely got the better of the other, though they had maintained the conflict for another two years, the war happened to be decided in quite a different manner. The two nations engaged were like well bred game-cocks that fight till their last gasp. You may see them often, when too weak to use their wings, yet full of pluck to the end and striking again and again. Finally chance brings them the opportunity of once more grappling, and they hold on until one or other of them drops down dead. (I, 58.)

So it was with the Romans and the Carthaginians. They were worn out by the labors of the war. The perpetual succession of hard fought struggles was at last driving them to despair; their strength had become paralyzed and their resources reduced almost to extinction by war taxes and expenses extending over so many years. And yet the Romans did not give in. For the last five years, indeed, they had entirely abandoned the sea, partly because of the disasters they had sustained and partly because they felt confident of deciding the war by means of their land forces; but they now determined for the third time to make trial of their fortune in naval warfare. . . . Nevertheless it was essentially an effort of despair. The treasury was empty and would not supply the funds necessary for the undertaking,—which were, however, obtained by the patriotism and generosity of the leading citizens. They undertook singly, or by two or three combining, according to their means, to supply a quinquereme fully fitted out, on the understanding that they were to be repaid if the expedition were successful. By these means a fleet of two hundred quinqueremes were quickly prepared, built on the model of the ship of the Rhodians. Gnaeus Lutatius was then appointed to the command and dispatched at the beginning of the summer. His appearance on the coast of Sicily was a surprise; the whole of the Carthaginian fleet had gone home, and he took possession both of the harbor near Drepana and the roadsteads near Lilybaeum. He then threw up works around the city of Drepana and made other preparations for besieging it. And while he pushed on these operations with all his might he did not at the same time lose sight of the approach of the Carthaginian fleet. He kept in mind the original idea of this expedition, that it was by a victory at sea alone that the result of the whole war could be decided. He did not, therefore, allow the time to be wasted or unemployed. He practiced and drilled his crews every day in the manoeuvers which they would be called upon to perform, and by his attention to discipline generally brought his sailors in a very short time to the conditions of trained athletes for the contest before them. (I, 59.)

That the Romans should have a fleet afloat once more and be again bidding for the mastery was a contingency wholly unexpected by the Carthaginians. (I, 60.)

When the Carthaginians saw that the Romans were intercepting their passage across they lowered their masts and, after some words of mutual exhortation had been uttered in the several ships, closed with their opponents. But the respective state of equipment of the two sides was exactly the converse of what it had been in the battle of Drepana, and the result of the battle was, therefore, naturally reversed also. The Romans had reformed their mode of shipbuilding and had eased their vessels of all freight, except the provisions necessary for the battle; while their rowers, having been thoroughly trained and got well together, performed their office in an altogether superior manner, and were backed up by marines who, being picked from the legions, were all but invincible. The case with the Carthaginians was exactly the reverse. Their ships were heavily laden, and therefore unmanageable in the engagement; while their rowers were entirely untrained and merely put on board for the emergency, and such marines as they had were raw recruits who had never had any previous experience of any difficult or dangerous service. The fact is that the Carthaginian government never expected that the Roman would again attempt to dispute the supremacy at sea. They had, therefore, in contempt for them, neglected their navy. The result was that, as soon as they had closed, their manifold disadvantages quickly decided the battle against them. They had fifty ships sunk and seventy taken with their crews. The rest set their sails and, running before the wind, which, luckily for them, suddenly veered around at the nick of time to help them, got away again to Holy Isle. The Roman consul sailed back to Lilybaeum to join the army, and there occupied himself in making arrangements for the ships and men which he had captured, which was a business of considerable magnitude, for the prisoners made in battle amounted to little short of ten thousand. (I, 61.)

QUESTIONS.

1. Prove the desperate character of the Carthaginian war. 2. Show how it was that Rome finally won; enumerate all the good features of the Roman constitution, the Roman military system, leadership, or character that enabled them to win in this supreme moment. 3. Draw a pen-picture of the Roman of this period, making use of all the answers given to the preceding questions.

ROMAN LIFE
OF THE
JUGURTHINE PERIOD.

CHAPTER VIII.

ROMAN LIFE OF THE JUGURTHINE PERIOD.

Sallust. Literally translated by the Rev. John Selby Watson, M. A. London, 1889.

Cicero, Marcus Tullius: The Orations of. Literally translated by C. D. Yonge, B. A. 4 vols. London, 1890. Vol. 1 used in extracts.

THE title for this study is not, perhaps, broad enough to cover all the extracts included under it. The original intention was to present material only from the Jugurthine period, but I have thought best to add a few extracts from Cicero's speech against Verres, delivered some thirty-five years after the close of the war, as evidence that the condition of Rome had not improved since Jugurtha's day.

Sallust, who wrote the history of the Jugurthine war, was not a contemporary writer. The war broke out 112 B. C. and Sallust was not born until 87 B. C., thus making him a contemporary of Cicero. Sallust served under Caesar as pro-consul in Numidia, and it was probably after the death of Caesar (44 B. C.) that the history of the Jugurthine war was written. If this date is correct, the history was composed about sixty years after the close of the war. It is not, then, the work of any eye witness, not even of a contemporary; the information is all derived, with the exception of a knowledge of the theatre of the war obtained from a residence in the country. In spite of all this, our information concerning this war is drawn chiefly from Sallust. His history is not a source, but, unfortunately, in the absence of sources, we can do no better than accept his work in place of the source. Perhaps no better illustration could be given of the uncertain foundation upon which our knowledge of the past sometimes rests.

What is the value of Sallust's History? Mommsen (Roman History, III, 198), says of it: "Sallust's political *genre*-painting of the Jugurthine war,—the only picture that has preserved its colors fresh in the utterly faded and blanched tradition of this epoch,—closes with the fall of Jugurtha, faithful to its style of composition,—poetical, not historical." In another place (III, 187) he writes: "In the fascinating and clever description of this war by Sallust the chronology has been unduly neglected." What we know of the man does not strengthen our confidence in his work. He is charged with licentiousness and corruption. He plundered Numidia, and on his return to Rome, he was followed by the Numidians, who charged him with extortion. Caesar interposed in his behalf. Seldom does he cite his sources of information, and his method of treatment does not justify us in concluding that he used them critically or followed them closely. The speeches, so frequently introduced, are clearly nothing more than so many rhetorical exercises.

The speech of Cicero presents material of a different kind. It was actually delivered in Rome in the year 70 B. C., in the prosecution of Verres for rapacity and tyranny while praetor in Sicily. Cicero was invited by the people of Sicily to prosecute Verres. He went there to collect evidence and, in his own words (Oration, chap. II), "I, in fifty days, so travelled over the whole of Sicily that I examined into the records and injuries of all the tribes and of all private individuals." The evidence was so overwhelming that Verres went of his own accord into banishment without trying to make a defense.

This speech then—due allowance being made for the fact that it was delivered in a public prosecution—would seem to contain the best of evidence upon the treatment of the provinces by such men as Verres. How far it would be safe to generalize upon this evidence is another question. All the Roman officials were certainly not so bad as Verres, but it is very clear that the opportunity for plunder existed and was taken advantage of to such an extent that it turned the provinces against Rome.

An excellent exercise in connection with this study would be to make use of Cicero's oration against Catiline as additional evidence. The Latin oration could be used when the class is made up of students that have already read the oration. When only a few in the class have read it they might be asked to present portions of it, emphasis being laid upon the fact that in using the Latin itself they are coming one step nearer to the event. Extracts from the Gallic Wars of Caesar might be used in the same way by classes studying Roman history.

I. The Jugurthine War.

JUGURTHA BRIBES INFLUENTIAL ROMANS.

The report of so atrocious an outrage (the murder of Hiempsal) was soon spread throughout Africa. Fear seized on Adherbal, and on all who had been subject to Micipsa. The Numidians divided into two parties, the greater number following Adherbal, but the more warlike, Jugurtha; who, accordingly, armed as large a force as he could, brought several cities, partly by force and partly by their own consent, under his power, and prepared to make himself sovereign of the whole of Numidia. Adherbal, though he had sent ambassadors to Rome, to inform the Senate of his brother's murder and his own circumstances, yet, relying on the number of his troops, prepared for an armed resistance. When the matter, however, came to a contest, he was defeated, and fled from the field of battle into our province, and from thence hastened to Rome.

Jugurtha, having thus accomplished his purposes, and reflecting, at leisure, on the crime which he had committed, began to feel a dread of the Roman people, against whose resentment he had no hopes of security but in the avarice of the nobility, and in his own wealth. A few days afterwards, therefore, he dispatched ambassadors to Rome, with a profusion of gold and silver, whom he directed, in the first place, to make an abundance of presents to his old friends, and then to procure him new ones; and not to hesitate, in short, to effect whatever could be done by bribery.

When these deputies had arrived at Rome, and had sent large presents, according to the prince's direction, to his intimate friends, and to others whose influence was at that time powerful, so remarkable a change ensued that Jugurtha, from being an object of the greatest odium, grew into great regard and favor with the nobility, who, partly allured with hope, and partly with actual largesses, endeavored, by soliciting the members of the Senate individually, to prevent any severe measures from being adopted against him. When the ambassadors, accordingly, felt sure of success, the Senate, on a fixed day, gave audience to both parties. (Chap. 13.)

QUESTIONS.

1. How did the Numidians evidently look upon Rome? 2. What advantages had Jugurtha over Adherbal? 3. What was evidently Jugurtha's opinion of the integrity of Roman leaders? 4. What reasons had he for such a belief? 5. Describe his methods in Rome. 6. Did their success bear out his belief?

JUGURTHA DEFENDS HIMSELF WITH BRIBES.

When the Prince Adherbal had concluded his speech, the ambassadors of Jugurtha, depending more on their money than their cause, replied, in a few words, "that Hiempsal had been put to death by the Numidians for his cruelty; that Adherbal, commencing war of his own accord, complained, after he was defeated, of being unable to do injury; and that Jugurtha entreated the Senate not to consider him a different person from what he had been known to be at Numantia, nor to set the assertions of his enemy above his own conduct."

Both parties then withdrew from the Senate house, and the Senate immediately proceeded to deliberate. The partisans of the ambassadors, with a great many others, corrupted by their influence, expressed contempt for the statements of Adherbal, extolled with the highest encomiums the merits of Jugurtha, and exerted themselves as strenuously with their interest and their eloquence, in defense of the guilt and infamy of another, as they would have striven for their own honor. A few, however, on the other hand, to whom right and justice were of more estimation than wealth, gave their opinion that Adherbal should be assisted, and the murder of Hiempsal should be severely avenged. Of all these the most forward was Aemilius Scaurus, a man of noble birth and great energy, but factious, and ambitious of power, honor, and wealth; yet an artful concealer of his own vices. He, seeing that the bribery of Jurgutha was notorious and shameless, and fearing that, as in such cases often happens, its scandalous profusion might excite public odium, restrained himself from the indulgence of his ruling passion. (Chap. 15.)

Yet that party gained the superiority in the Senate, which preferred money and interest to justice. A decree was made "that ten commissioners should divide the kingdom, which Micipsa had possessed, between Jugurtha and Adherbal." Of this commission, the leading person was Lucius Opimius, a man of distinction and of great influence at that time in the Senate, from having in his Consulship on the death of Caius Gracchus and Marcus Falvius Flaccus, prosecuted the victory of the nobility over the plebians with great severity.

Jugurtha, though he had already counted Scaurus among his friends at Rome, yet received him with the most studied ceremony, and by presents and promises, wrought on him so effectually that he preferred the prince's interest to his own character, honor, and all other considerations. The rest of the commissioners he assailed in a similar way and gained over most of them; by a few only integrity was more regarded than lucre. - In the division of the kingdom, that part of Numidia which borders on Mauretania, and which is superior in fertility and population, was allotted to Jugurtha; of the other part, which, though better furnished with harbors and buildings, was more valuable in appearance than in reality, Adherbal became the possessor. (Chap. 16.)

QUESTIONS.

1. Apart from the murder of Hiempsal, what charges could really be made against Jugurtha? 2. Was his defense skilfully conducted? 3. To what extent do the facts given by Sallust bear out his generalizations? 4. Upon what points is more first hand evidence necessary? 5. What statements would it be difficult, under the most favorable conditions, to prove?

THE SENATE CORRUPTED BY JUGURTHA.

These deputies soon arrived in Africa, using the greater dispatch, because, whilst they were preparing for their journey, a report was spread in Rome of the battle which had been fought and of the siege of Cirta; but this report told much less than the truth. Jugurtha, having given them an audience, replied, "that nothing was of greater weight with him, nothing more respected, than the authority of the Senate; that it had been his endeavor, from his youth, to deserve the esteem of all men of worth; that he had gained the favor of Publius Scipio, a man of the highest eminence, not by dishonorable practices, but by merit; that, for the same good qualities, and not from want of heirs to the throne, he had been adopted by Micipsa; but that, the more honorable and spirited his conduct had been, the less could his feelings endure injustice; that Adherbal had formed designs against his life, on discovering which, he had counteracted his malice; that the Romans would act neither justly nor reasonably if they withheld from him the common right of nations; and, in conclusion, that he would soon send ambassadors to Rome to explain the whole of his proceedings." On this understanding, both parties separated. Of addressing Adherbal, the deputies had no opportunity. (Chap. 22.)

When this outrage was reported at Rome, and became a matter of discussion in the Senate, the former partisans of Jugurtha applied themselves by interrupting the debates and protracting the time, sometimes exerting their interests, and sometimes quarreling wi h particular members, to palliate the atrocity of the deed. And had not Caius Memmius, one of the tribunes of the people elect, convinced the people of Rome that an attempt was being made, by the agency of a small faction, to have the crimes of Jugurtha pardoned, it is certain that the public indignation against him would have passed off under the protraction of the debates; so powerful was party interest and the influence of Jugurtha's mon y. (Chap. 27.)

QUESTIONS.

1. Does Jugurtha's speech to the ambassadors seem plausible? 2. Upon what one point would you like more evidence? 3. Concerning what took place in Rome, what two things would be generally known? 4. Would it have been even then so easy to prove the causes of the delay in the Senate? 5. Our belief in the corruption of the Senate rests upon what other belief?

JUGURTHA BRIBES A CONSUL AND CORRUPTS HIS ARMY.

When Jugurtha received this news (that an army was to be sent against him) which was utterly at variance with his expectations, as he had felt convinced that all things were purchasable at Rome, he sent his son, with two of his friends, as deputies to the Senate, and directed them, like those whom he had sent on the murder of Hiempsal, to attack everybody with bribes. (Chap. 28.)

But when Jugurtha began to tempt him (Calpurnius, the Consul) with bribes, and to show the difficulties of the war which he had undertaken to conduct, his mind, corrupted with avarice, was easily altered. His accomplice, however, and manager in all his schemes, was Scaurus; who, though he had at first, when most of his party were corrupted, displayed violent hostility to Jugurtha, yet was afterwards seduced by a vast sum of money from integrity and honor to injustice and perfidy. (Chap. 29.)

During the course of these proceedings at Rome, those whom Bestia had left in Numidia in command of the army, following the example of their general, had been guilty of many scandalous transactions. Some, seduced by gold, had restored Jugurtha his elephants; others had sold him his deserters; others had ravished the lands of those at peace with us; so strong a spirit of rapacity, like the contagion of pestilence, had pervaded the breasts of all. (Chap. 32.)

QUESTIONS.

1. How many of the statements made by Sallust in chapter 28 would it have been difficult to prove even at the time? 2. What easily ascertainable fact is stated in the same chapter? 3. What was evidently the belief in Rome concerning the integrity of Calpurnius and Scaurus? 4. What was the condition of the army in Africa?

JUGURTHA BRIBES A TRIBUNE.

Jugurtha, accordingly, accompanied Cassius to Rome, but without any mark of royalty, and in the garb, as much as possible, of a suppliant; and, though he felt great confidence on his own part, and was supported by all those through whose power or villany he had accomplished his projects, he purchased, by a vast bribe, the aid of Caius Baebius, a tribune of the people, by whose audacity he hoped to be protected against the law and against all harm. (Chap. 33.)

But when Memmius had concluded his speech, and Jugurtha was expected to give his answer, Caius Baebius, the tribune of the people, whom I have just noticed as having been bribed, enjoined the prince to hold his peace; and though the multitude, who formed the assembly, were desperately enraged, and endeavored to terrify the tribune by outcries, by angry looks, by violent gestures, and by every other act to which anger prompts, his audacity was at last triumphant. The people, mocked and set at naught, withdrew from the place of assembly; and the confidence of Jugurtha, Baestia, and the others, whom this investigation had alarmed, was greatly augmented. (Chap. 34.)

QUESTIONS.

1. What reason had Jugurtha to feel confident? 2. Why did he then wear "the garb of a suppliant"? 3. What proof does Sulla give that the tribune Baebius was bribed by Jugurtha? 4. What influence did the people of Rome have at this time?

THE ASSASSINATION OF MASSIVA.

One of their number sprung upon Massiva, though with too little caution, and killed him; but being himself caught, he made, at the instigation of many, and especially of Albinus the consul, a full confession. Bomilcar was accordingly committed for trial, though rather on the principles of reason and justice than in accordance with the law of nations, as he was in the retinue of one who had come to Rome on a pledge of the public faith for his safety. But Jugurtha, though clearly guilty of the crime, did not cease to struggle against the truth until he perceived that the infamy of the deed was too strong for his interests or his money; for which reason, although, at the commencement of the proceedings he had given fifty of his friends as bail for Bomilcar, yet, thinking more of his kingdom than of the sureties, he sent him off privately into Numidia; for he feared that if such a man should be executed, his other subjects would be deterred from obeying him. A few days after, he himself departed, having been ordered by the Senate to quit Italy. But, as he was going from Rome, he is said, after frequently looking back on it in silence, to have at last exclaimed: "That it was a venal city, and would soon perish if it could but find a purchaser!" (Chap. 35.)

QUESTIONS.

1. Why was it not "in accordance with the law of nations" that Bomilcar should be tried? 2. Give a list of the acts committed by Jugurtha that showed his lawlessness. 3. Ranke believes that Jugurtha must have spoken the famous words before leaving Rome. Why should he think so?

LACK OF DISCIPLINE IN THE ARMY.

Meanwhile, by means of skillful emissaries, he tampered night and day with our men, and prevailed on some of the officers, both of infantry and cavalry, to desert to him at once and upon others to quit their posts at a given signal, that their defection might thus be less observed. Having prepared matters according to his wishes, he suddenly surrounded the camp of Aulus in the dead of night, with a vast body of Numidians. The Roman soldiers were alarmed with an unusual disturbance; some of them seized their arms, others hid themselves, others encouraged those that were afraid; but consternation prevailed everywhere; for the number of the enemy was great, the sky was thick with clouds and darkness, the danger was indiscernible, and it was uncertain whether it was safer to flee or to remain. Of those whom I have just mentioned as being bribed, one cohort of Ligurians, with two troops of Thracian horse, and a few common soldiers, went over to Jugurtha; and the chief centurion of the third legion allowed the enemy an entrance which he had been appointed to defend, and at which all the Numidians poured into the camp. Our men fled disgracefully, the greater part having thrown their arms, and took possession of a neighboring hill. (Chap. 38.)

QUESTIONS.

1. Contrast the conduct of the Romans in this war with their conduct in the Carthaginian war. What changes have taken place? 2. What change has taken place in the composition of the army? 3. What influence would that be likely to have?

CORRUPTION IN THE GOVERNMENT AND LACK OF MILITARY VIRTUE IN THE ARMY.

The prevalence of parties among the people, and the factions in the Senate, and of all evil practices dependent on them, had its origin at Rome a few years before, during a period of tranquillity, and amidst the abundance of all that mankind regarded as desirable. For, before the destruction of Carthage, the Senate and the people managed the affairs of the Republic with mutual moderation and forbearance; there were no contests among the citizens for honor or ascendency; but the dread of an enemy kept the state in order. When that fear, however, was removed from their minds, licentiousness and pride, evils which prosperity loves to foster, immediately began to prevail; and thus peace, which they had so eagerly desired in adversity, proved, when they had obtained it, more grievous and fatal than adversity itself. The patricians carried their authority and the people their liberty to excess; every man took, snatched, and seized what he could. There was a complete division into two factions, and the Republic was torn into pieces between them. Yet the nobility still maintained an ascendency by conspiring together; for the strength of the people, being disunited and dispersed among a multitude, was less able to exert itself. Things were accordingly directed, both at home and in the field, by the will of a small number of men, at whose disposal were the treasuries, the provinces, offices, honors, and triumphs; while the people were oppressed with military service and with poverty, and the generals divided the spoils of war with a few of their friends. (Chap. 41.)

When he arrived in Africa, the command of the army was assigned to him by Albinus, the pro-consul; but it was an army spiritless and unwarlike; incapable of encountering either danger or fatigue; more ready with the tongue than with the sword; accustomed to plunder our allies while itself was the prey of the enemy; unchecked by discipline, and void of respect to its character. The new general, accordingly, felt more anxiety from the corrupt morals of the men, than confidence or hope from their numbers. He determined, however, though the delay of the commitia had shortened his summer campaign, and though he knew his countrymen to be anxious for the result of the proceedings, not to commence operations, until, by the revival of the old discipline he had brought the soldiers to bear fatigue. . . . But neither had the camp been fortified, nor the watches kept according to military usage; everyone had been allowed to leave his post when he pleased. The camp followers mingled with the soldiers, wandered about day and night, ravaging the country, robbing the houses, and vieing with each other in carrying off cattle and slaves which they exchanged with traders for foreign wine and other luxuries; they even sold the corn, which was given them from the public store and bought bread from day to day. (Chap. 44.)

QUESTIONS.

1. Enumerate all the evils in Roman society that are shown by Sallust. 2. How many of his statements deal with the matters that must have been clear to the public at large? 3. How many of his statements are detailed and proved? 4. What changes had taken place in the army?

II. Maladministration of Provinces.

THE JUDGES CORRUPT.

For an opinion has now become established, pernicious to us, and pernicious to the public, which has been the common talk of everyone, not only of Rome, but among foreign nations also—that in the courts of law as they exist at present no wealthy man, however guilty he may be, can possibly be convicted. Now, at this time of peril to your order, and to your tribunals, when men are ready to attempt by harangues and by the proposal of new laws, to increase the existing unpopularity of the Senate, Caius Verres is brought to trial as a criminal, a man condemned in the opinion of everyone by his life and actions, but acquitted by the enormousness of his wealth, according to his own hope and boast. I, O Judges, have undertaken this cause as prosecutor with the greatest good wishes and expectation on the part of the Roman people, not in order to increase the unpopularity of the Senate, but to relieve it from the discredit which I share with it. For I have brought before you a man, by acting justly in whose case, you have an opportunity of retrieving the lost credit of your judicial proceedings, of regaining your credit with the Roman people, and of giving satisfaction to foreign nations; a man, the embezzler of the public funds, the petty tyrant of Asia and Pamphylia, the robber who would deprive the city of its rights, the disgrace and ruin of the province of Sicily. And if you come to a decision about this man with severity, and a due regard to your oaths, that authority which ought to remain in you will cling to you still, but if that man with vast riches shall break down the sanctity of the courts of justice, at least I shall achieve this, that it shall be plain that it was rather honest judgment that was wanting to the republic than a criminal to the judges or an accuser to the criminal. (Chap. 1.)

While this man was praetor, the Sicilians enjoyed neither their own laws nor the decrees of our Senate, nor the common rights of every nation. Everyone in Sicily has only so much left as either escaped the notice or was desregarded by the satiety of that most avaricious and licentious man. (Chap. 4.)

No legal decision for three years was given on any other ground but his will; no property was so secure to any man, even if it had descended to him from his father and grandfather, but he was deprived of it at his command; enormous sums of money were exacted from the property of the cultivators of the soil by a new and nefarious system. The most faithful of the allies were classed in the number of enemies. Roman citizens were tortured and put to death like slaves; the greatest criminals were acquitted in the courts of justice through bribery; the most upright and honorable men, being prosecuted while absent, were condemned and banished without being heard in their own defense; the most fortified harbors, the greatest and strongest cities, were laid open to pirates and robbers; the sailors and soldiers of the Sicilians, our own allies and friends, died of hunger; the best built fleets on the most important stations were lost and destroyed, to the great disgrace of the Roman people. This same man while praetor plundered and stripped those most ancient monuments, some erected by wealthy monarchs and intended by them as ornaments for their cities; some, too, the work of our own generals, which they either gave or restored as conquerors to the different states in Sicily. And he did this not only to public statues and ornaments, but he also plundered all the temples consecrated in the deepest religious feelings of the people. He did not leave, in short, one god to the Sicilians which appeared to him to be made in a tolerably workmanlike manner, and with any of the skill of the ancients. (Oration, chap. 5.)

QUESTIONS.

1. Compare the value of this material with that taken from Sallust. 2. What evidence does Cicero give of the corrupt state of the courts? 3. What interest had "foreign nations" in this trial? 4. Enumerate the crimes committed by Verres and show how the state would be injured by them.

VERRES TRIES TO CORRUPT THE COURT.

When he first returned from the province, he endeavored to get rid of this prosecution by corrupting the judges at a great expense; and this object he continued to keep in view till the conclusion of the appointment of the judges. After the judges were appointed, because in drawing lots for them the fortune of the Roman people had defeated his hopes, and in rejecting some, my diligence had defeated his impudence, before the attempted bribery was abandoned. The affair was going on admirably; lists of your names and of the whole tribunal were in everyone's hands. It did not seem possible to mark the votes of these men with any distinguishing mark or color or spot of dirt; and that fellow, from having been brisk and in high spirits, became on a sudden so downcast and humbled that he seemed to be condemned not only by the Roman people, but even by himself. But lo! all of a sudden, within these few days, since the consular commitia has taken place, he has gone back to his original plan with more money, and his same plots are now laid against your reputation and against the fortunes of everyone, by the instrumentality of the same people. (Chap. 6.)

For as Hortensius, the consul elect, was being attended home again from the campus by a great concourse and multitude of people, Caius Curio fell in with that multitude by chance,—a man whom I wish to name by way of honor rather than by way of disparagement. I will tell you what, if he had been unwilling to have it mentioned, he would not have spoken of in so large an assembly, so openly and undisguisedly; which, however, shall be mentioned by me deliberately and cautiously that it may be seen that I pay due regard to our friendship and to his dignity. He sees Verres in a crowd by the Arch of Fabius; he speaks to the man, and with a loud voice congratulates him on his victory. He does not say a word to Hortensius himself, who had been made consul, or to his friends and relations who were present attending on him; but he stops to speak to this man, embraces him, and bids him cast off all anxiety. "I give you notice," said he, "that you have been acquitted by this day's commitia." And as many most honorable men heard this it is immediately reported to me; indeed, everyone who saw me mentioned it to me the first thing. To some it appeared scandalous, to others ridiculous; ridiculous to those who thought that this cause depended on the credibility of the witnesses, on the importance of the charges, and on the power of the judges, and not on the consular commitia; scandalous to those who looked deeper, and who thought that this congratulation had reference to the corruption of the judge. In truth they argued in this manner—the most honorable men spoke to one another and to me in this manner—that there were now manifestly and undeniably no courts of justice at all. The very criminal who the day before thought that he was already condemned, is acquitted now that his defender has been made consul. What are we to think then? Will it avail nothing that all Sicily, all the Sicilians, that all the merchants who have business in that country, that all public and private documents are now at Rome? Nothing, if the consul elect wills it otherwise. What! Will not the judges be influenced by the accusation, by the evidence, by the universal opinion of the Roman people? No. Everything will be governed by the power and authority of one man. (Oration, chap. 7.)

QUESTIONS.

1. How did Cicero defeat Verres' attempt at bribery? 2. Why did Verres use his money to elect Hortensius? 3. Why did Cicero consider the conversation between Curio and Verres so important? 4. What was the real danger that menaced the Roman state? 5. Make a brief comparison of the Roman of this period with the Roman of the preceding period.

ROMAN LIFE UNDER THE EMPIRE.

CHAPTER IX.

ROMAN LIFE UNDER THE EMPIRE.

The Letters of Caius Plinius Caecilius Secundus. The translation of Melmoth, revised and corrected by Rev. F. C. Bosanquet, B. A. London, 1890.

PLINY, commonly known as Pliny the younger, was born 62 A. D. On the death of his father he was adopted by his uncle, the elder Pliny. He received a careful education, being a pupil of the famous Quintilian. He practiced for some time at the Roman bar, then entered public life. After holding the offices of military tribune, quaestor, praetor, and consul, he was sent as pro-praetor to Pontica by the Emperor Trajan. It was during his residence in this province (102-103 A. D.) that the most of the correspondence, from which I quote, passed between him and the emperor.

The collection of letters from which these are chosen was published by Pliny during his lifetime. In the first letter he writes to Septitius as follows: "You have frequently pressed me to make a select collection of my letters (if there really be any deserving of a special preference) and give them to the public. I have selected them accordingly; not, indeed, in their proper order of time, for I was not compiling a history, but just as each came to hand."

I have made no extracts from the great number of letters dealing with Pliny's private life, but have confined my selections to his correspondence as governor of Pontica. This is the best material that has yet been published in the Studies. Perhaps the next best material is the description of the Roman constitution as given by Polybius. But there is a marked difference between the histories of Polybius and the letters of Pliny; Polybius is consciously describing a government and Pliny is not. The letters of Pliny and Trajan are parts of the government machinery and teach us, by inference, much that they did not intend to teach.

At the close of this study a most interesting comparison might be made between the Roman constitution in the two phases of development shown by Polybius and Pliny.

PLINY TO TRAJAN.

I was greatly obliged, Sir, in my late illness, to Posthumius Marinus, my physician; and I cannot make him a suitable return, but by the assistance of your wonted gracious indulgence. I entreat you, then, to make Chrysippus Mithridates and his wife Stratonica (who are related to Marinus) denizens of Rome. 1 entreat likewise the same privilege in favor of Epigonus and Mithridates, the two sons of Chrysippus; but with this restriction, that they may remain under the dominion of their father, and yet preserve their right of patronage over their own freedmen. I further entreat you to grant the full privileges of a Roman to L. Satrius Abascantius, P. Caesius Phosphorus, and Pancharia Soteris. This request I make with the consent of their patrons. (Bk. X, Letter X.)

PLINY TO TRAJAN.

After your late sacred father, Sir, had, in a noble speech, as well as by his own generous example, exhorted and encouraged the public to acts of munificence, I implored his permission to remove the several statues which I had of the former emperors to my corporation, and at the same time requested permission to add his own to the number. For as I had hitherto let them remain in the respective places in which they stood when they were left to me by several different inheritances, they were dispersed in different parts of my estate. He was pleased to grant my request, and at the same time to give me a very ample testimony of his approbation. I immediately, therefore, wrote to the decurii,* to desire they would allot a piece of ground, upon which I might build a temple at my own expense; and they, as a mark of honour to my design, offered me the choice of any site I might think proper. However, my own ill-health in the first place, and later that of your father, together with the duties of that employment which you were both pleased to trust me, prevented my proceeding with that design. But I have now, I think, a convenient opportunity of making an excursion for that purpose, as my monthly attendance ends on the 1st of September, and there are several festivals in the month following. My first request, then, is that you would permit me to adorn the temple I am going to erect with your statue, and next (in order to the execution of my design with all the expedition possible) that you would indulge me with leave of absence. It would ill become the sincerity I profess, were I to dissemble that your goodness in complying with this desire will at the same time be extremely serviceable to me in my own private affairs. It is absolutely necessary I should not defer any longer the letting of my lands in that province; for, besides that they amount to above four hundred thousand sesterces, the time for dressing the vineyards is approaching, and that business must fall upon my new tenants. The unfruitfulness of the seasons besides, for several years past, obliges me to think of making some abatements in my rents; which I cannot possibly settle unless I am present. I shall be indebted then to your indulgence, Sir, for the expedition of my work of piety, and the settlement of my own private affairs, if you will be pleased to grant me leave of absence for thirty days. I cannot give myself a shorter time, as the town and estate of which I am speaking lie above a hundred and fifty miles from Rome. (Bk. X, Letter XI.)

QUESTIONS.

1. How is the power of the Emperor shown in Letter X? 2. What would you think of Pliny, if you judged him from this letter? 3. Enumerate all the different classes referred to in Letter X and indicate the relations existing among them. 4. What two kinds of favors does Pliny ask in the first letter and which was

---

* Members of the senate or council of a city.

the more valuable? 5. Were these privileges valuable? 6. What is there peculiar about Pliny's request touching the statues (Letter XI)? 7. What does the second part of Letter XI tell us about the ability and character of Pliny?

TRAJAN TO PLINY.

You have given me many private reasons, and every public one, why you desire leave of absence; but I need no other than that it is your desire; and I doubt not of your returning as soon as possible to the duty of an office which so much requires your attendance. As I would not seem to check any instance of your affection towards me, I shall not oppose your erecting my statue in the place you desire; though in general I am extremely cautious in giving any encouragement to honours of that kind. (Bk. X, Letter XII.)

PLINY TO TRAJAN.

As I am sensible, Sir, that the highest applause my actions can receive is to be distinguished by so excellent a prince, I beg you would be graciously pleased to add either the office of augur or septemvir* (both which are now vacant) to the dignity I already enjoy by your indulgence; that I may have the satisfaction of publicly offering up those vows for your prosperity, from the duty of my office, which I prefer to the gods in private, from the affection of my heart. (Bk. X, Letter XIII.)

PLINY TO TRAJAN.

Having safely passed the promontory of Malea, I am arrived at Ephesus with all my retinue, notwithstanding I was detained for some time by contrary winds; a piece of information, Sir, in which, I trust, you will feel yourself concerned. I propose pursuing the remainder of my journey to the province partly in light vessels, and partly in post-chaises; for, as the excessive heats will prevent my traveling altogether by land, so the Etesian† winds, which are now set in, will not permit me to proceed entirely by sea. (Bk. X, Letter XIV.)

---

*One of seven priests.
† A north wind.

PLINY TO TRAJAN.

As I had a very favorable voyage to Ephesus, so in traveling by post-chaise from thence I was extremely troubled by the heat, and also by some slight feverish attacks, which kept me for some time at Pergamus. From there, Sir, I got on board a coasting vessel, but, being again detained by contrary winds, did not arrive at Bithynia so soon as I had hoped. However, I have no reason to complain of this delay, since (which, indeed, was the most auspicious circumstance that could attend me) I reached the province in time to celebrate your birthday. I am at present engaged in examining the finances of the Prusenses, their expenses, revenues, and credits; and the farther I proceed in this work, the more I am convinced of the necessity of my enquiry. Several large sums of money are owing to the city from private persons, which they neglect to pay upon various pretences; as, on the other hand, I find the public funds are, in some instances, very unwarrantly applied. This, Sir, I write to you immediately on my arrival. I entered this province on the 17th of September, and found in it that obedience and loyalty towards yourself which you justly merit from all mankind. You will consider, Sir, whether it would not be proper to send a surveyor here; for I am inclined to think much might be deducted from what is charged by those who have the conduct of the public works if a faithful admeasurement were to be taken; at least I am of that opinion from what I have already seen of the accounts of this city, which I am now going into as fully as is possible. (Bk. X, Letter XVI.)

QUESTIONS.

1. What idea do you form of Trajan's character from Letter XII? 2. What modern political feature appears in Letter XIII? 3. Trace the voyage of Pliny (Letters XIV, XV) and compare the modes of travel in his day with those in our own. 4. What was the situation of the province? 5. Was Pliny a good man for the place?

PLINY TO TRAJAN.

Though I am well assured, Sir, that you, who never omit any opportunity of exerting your generosity, are not unmindful of the request I lately made to you, yet, as you have often indulged me in this manner, give me leave to remind and earnestly entreat you to bestow the praetorship now vacant upon Attius Sura. Though his ambition is extremely moderate, yet the quality of his birth, the inflexible integrity he has preserved in a very narrow fortune, and, more than all, the felicity of your times, which encourages conscious virtue to claim your favour, induce him to hope he may experience it in the present instance. (Bk. X, Letter XVIII.)

QUESTIONS.

1. When have you met with requests similar to the above?

PLINY TO TRAJAN.

Your generosity to me, Sir, was the occasion of uniting me to Rosianus Geminus by the strongest ties; for he was my quaestor when I was consul. His behavior to me during the continuance of our offices was highly respectful, and he has treated me ever since with so peculiar a regard that, besides the many obligations I owe him upon a public account, I am indebted to him for the strongest pledges of private friendship. I entreat you, then, to comply with my request for the advancement of one whom (if my recommendation has any weight) you will even distinguish with your particular favour; and whatever trust you shall repose in him, he will endeavour to show himself still deserving of an higher. But I am the more sparing in my praises of him, being persuaded his integrity, his probity, and his vigilance are well known to you, not only from those high posts which he has exercised in Rome within your immediate inspection, but from his behaviour when he served under you in the army. One thing, however, my affection for him inclines me to think, I have not sufficiently done; and therefore, Sir, I repeat my entreaties that you will give me the pleasure, as early as possible, of rejoicing in the advancement of my quaestor, or, in other words, of receiving an addition to my own honours, in the person of my friend. (Bk. X, Letter XXI.)

QUESTIONS.

1. What danger to the empire lies in the power of the Emperor to grant requests like those made for himself and his friends by Pliny?

PLINY TO TRAJAN.

I am informed by a letter from the king of Sarmatia that there are certain affairs of which you ought to be informed as soon as possible. In order, therefore, to hasten the dispatches which his courier was charged with to you, I granted him an order to make use of the public post. (Bk. X, Letter XXIV.)

QUESTIONS.

1. What was this "public post" (see Letters CXXI, CXXII)? 2. Why should Pliny mention so unimportant a matter?

PLINY TO TRAJAN.

I beg your determination, Sir, on a point I am exceedingly doubtful about: it is whether I should place the public slaves as sentries round the prisons of the several cities of this province (as has hitherto been the practice) or employ a party of soldiers for that purpose? On the one hand, I am afraid the public slaves will not attend this duty with the fidelity they ought; and on the other, that it will engage too large a body of the soldiery. In the meanwhile I have joined a few of the latter with the former. I am apprehensive, however, there may be some danger that this method will occasion a general neglect of duty, as it will afford them a mutual opportunity of throwing the blame upon each other. (Bk. X, Letter XXX.)

TRAJAN TO PLINY.

There is no occasion, my dearest Secundus, to draw off any soldiers in order to guard the prisons. Let us rather persevere in the ancient customs observed in this province of employing the slaves for that purpose; and the fidelity with which they shall execute their duty will depend upon your care and strict discipline. It is greatly to be feared, as you observe, if the soldiers should be mixed with the public slaves, they will mutually trust to each other, and by that means grow so much the more negligent. But my principal objection is that as few soldiers as possible should be withdrawn from their standard. (Bk. X, Letter XXXI.)

QUESTIONS.

1. Enumerate all the evils of Roman society as shown in Letters XXX, XXXI. 2. What difference between the attitude of Pliny and that of Trajan?

PLINY TO TRAJAN.

The Prusenses, Sir, having an ancient bath which lies in a ruinous state, desire your leave to repair it; but, upon examination, I am of opinion it ought to be rebuilt. I think, therefore, you may indulge them in this request, as there will be a sufficient fund for that purpose, partly from those debts which are due from private persons to the public which I am now collecting in; and partly from what they raise among themselves towards furnishing the bath with oil, which they are willing to apply to the carrying on of this building; a work which the dignity of the city and the splendour of your times seem to demand. (Bk. X, Letter XXXIV.)

TRAJAN TO PLINY.

If the erecting a public bath will not be too great a charge upon the Prusenses, we may comply with their request; provided, however, that no new tax be levied for this purpose, nor any of those taken off which are appropriated to necessary services. (Bk. X, Letter XXXV.)

QUESTIONS.

1. Why should the Emperor interfere in such a matter as the rebuilding of a bath?

PLINY TO TRAJAN.

The very excellent young man Sempronius Caelianus, having discovered two slaves among the recruits, has sent them to me. But I deferred passing sentence till I had consulted you, the restorer and upholder of military discipline, concerning the punishment proper to be inflicted upon them. My principal doubt is that, whether, although they have taken the military oath, they are yet entered into any particular legion. I request you, therefore, Sir, to inform me what course I should pursue in this affair, especially as it concerns example. (Bk. X, Letter XXXVIII.)

QUESTIONS.

1. What light does this letter throw upon the position of the slave? 2. Was Pliny a harsh governor?

TRAJAN TO PLINY.

You are of opinion it would be proper to establish

a company of fire-men in Nicomedia, agreeably to what has been practiced in other cities. But it is to be remembered that societies of this sort have greatly disturbed the peace of the province in general, and of those cities in particular. Whatever name we may give them, and for whatever purposes they may be founded, they will not fail to form themselves into factious assemblies, however short their meetings may be. It will therefore be safer to provide such machines as are of service in extinguishing fires, enjoining the owners of houses to assist in preventing the mischief from spreading, and, if it should be necessary, to call in the aid of the populace. (Bk. X, Letter XLIII.)

QUESTIONS.

1. Why should Pliny want to form a fire company? 2. Why should Trajan object? 3. Which was right? 4. Look back over the letters and point out other cases where the imperial point of view clashed with the provincial.

PLINY TO TRAJAN.

The citizens of Nicomedia, Sir, have expended three millions three hundred and twenty-nine sesterces in building an aqueduct; but, not being able to finish it, the works are entirely falling to ruin. They made a second attempt in another place, where they laid out two millions. But this likewise is discontinued; so that, after having been at an immense charge to no purpose, they must still be at a further expense, in order to be accommodated with water. I have examined a fine spring from whence the water may be conveyed over arches (as was attempted in their first design) in such a manner that the higher as well as level and low parts of the city may be supplied. There are still remaining a very few of the old arches; and the square stones, however, employed in the former building, may be used in turning the new arches. I am of opinion part should be raised with brick, as that will be the easier and cheaper material. But that this work may not meet with the same ill-success as the former, it will be necessary to send here an architect, or some one skilled in the construction of this kind of waterworks. And I will venture to say, from the beauty and usefulness of the design, it will be an erection well worthy the splendour of your times. (Bk. X, Letter XLVI.)

TRAJAN TO PLINY.

You, who are upon the spot, will best be able to consider and determine what is proper to be done concerning the theatre which the inhabitants of Nicea are building; as for myself, it will be sufficient if you let me know your determination. With respect to the particular parts of this theatre which are to be raised at a private charge, you will see those engagements fulfilled when the body of the building to which they are to be annexed shall be finished. These paltry Greeks are, I know, immoderately fond of gymnastic diversions, and therefore, perhaps, the citizens of Nicea have planned a more magnificent building for this purpose than is necessary; however, they must be content with such as will be sufficient to answer the purpose for which it is intended. I leave it entirely to you to persuade the Claudiopolitani as you shall think proper with regard to their bath, which they have placed, it seems, in a very improper situation. As there is no province that is not furnished with men of skill and ingenuity, you cannot possibly want architects; unless you think it the shortest way to procure them from Rome, when it is generally from Greece that they come to us. (Bk. X, Letter XLIX.)

QUESTIONS.

1. What good judgment does Trajan show in Letters XLVI, XLIX? 2. What is Trajan's opinion of the Greek? 3. What is the influence of Greece upon Rome?

PLINY TO TRAJAN.

Upon examining into the public expenses of the city of Byzantium, which, I find, are extremely great, I was informed, Sir, that the appointments of the ambassador whom they send yearly to you with their homage, and the decree which passes in the senate upon that occasion, amount to twelve thousand sesterces. But knowing the generous maxims of your government, I thought proper to send the decree without the ambassador, that, at the same time they discharged their public duty to you, their expense incurrred in the manner of paying it might be lightened. This city is likewise taxed with the sum of three thousand sesterces towards defraying the expense of an envoy, whom they annually send to compliment the governor of Moesia; this expense I have also directed to be spared. I beg, Sir, you would deign either to confirm my judgment or correct my error in these points, by acquainting me with your sentiments. (Bk. X, Letter LII.)

TRAJAN TO PLINY.

I entirely approve, my dearest Secundus, of your having excused the Byzantines that expense of twelve thousand sesterces in sending an ambassador to me. I shall esteem their duty as sufficiently paid, though I only receive the act of their senate through your hands. The governor of Moesia must likewise excuse them if they compliment him at a less expense. (Bk. X, Letter LIII.)

QUESTIONS.

1. What proof do you find in letters LII, LIII, that Trajan realized that it was his business to think of the people's welfare rather than his own glory?

PLINY TO TRAJAN.

Upon intimating, Sir, my intention to the city of Apamea of examining into the state of their public dues, their revenue, and expenses, they told me they were all extremely willing I should inspect their accounts, but that no proconsul had ever yet looked them over, as they had a privilege (and that of a very ancient date) of administering the affairs of their corporation in the manner they thought proper. I required them to draw up a memorial of what they then asserted, which I transmit to you precisely as I received it; though I am sensible it contains several things foreign to the question. I beg you will deign to instruct me as to how I am to act in this affair, for I should be extremely sorry either to exceed or fall short of the duties of my commission. (Bk. X, Letter LVI.)

TRAJAN TO PLINY.

The memorial of the Apameans annexed to your letter has saved me the necessity of considering the reasons they suggest why the former proconsuls forebore to inspect their accounts, since they are willing to sumbit them to your examination. Their honest compliance deserves to be rewarded; and they may be assured the inquiry you are to make in pursuance of my orders shall be with a full reserve to their privileges. (Bk. X, Letter LVII.)

QUESTIONS.

1. Were all cities absolutely subject to Rome? 2. Was Trajan jealous of his imperial rights?

PLINY TO TRAJAN.

The debts which were owing to the public are, by the prudence, Sir, of your counsels, and the care of my administration, either actually paid in or now being collected; but I am afraid the money must lie unemployed. For as on one side there are few or no opportunities of purchasing land, so, on the other, one cannot meet with any person who is willing to borrow of the public (especially at 12 per cent. interest) when they can raise money upon the same terms from private sources. You will consider, then, Sir, whether it may not be advisable, in order to invite responsible persons to take this money, to lower the interest; or if that scheme should not succeed, to place it in the hands of the decurii, upon their giving sufficient security to the public. And though they should not be willing to receive it, yet as the rate of interest will be diminished, the hardship will be so much the less. (Bk. X, Letter LXII.)

QUESTIONS.

1. What unwise policy was the government following in Pliny's province? 2. What does Pliny's letter tell us about the condition of the province?

TRAJAN TO PLINY.

I agree with you, my dear Pliny, that there seems to be no other method of facilitating the placing out of the public money than by lowering the interest; the measure of which you will determine according to the number of the borrowers. But to compel persons to receive it who are not disposed to do so, when possibly they themselves may have no opportunity of employing it, is, by no means, consistent with the justice of my government. (Bk. X, Letter LXIII.)

QUESTIONS.

1. Why would Pliny's plan have worked an injustice to the decurii?

PLINY TO TRAJAN.

A very considerable question, Sir, in which the whole province is interested, has been lately started concerning the state and maintenance of deserted children. I have examined the constitutions of former princes upon this head, but not finding anything in them relating, either in general or particular, to the Bithynians, I thought it necessary to apply to you for your directions; for in a point which seems to require the special interposition of your authority, I could not content myself with following precedents. An edict of the emperor Augustus (as pretended) was read to me concerning one Annia; as also a letter from Vespasian to the Lacedaemonians, and another from Titus to the same, with one likewise from him to the Achaeans, also some letters from Domitian, directed to the proconsuls Avidius Nigrimus and Armenius Brocchus, together with one from that prince to the Lacedaemonians; but I have not transmitted them to you, as they were not correct (and some of them, too, of doubtful authenticity), and also because I imagine the true copies are preserved in your archives. (Bk. X, Letter LXXI.)

TRAJAN TO PLINY.

The question concerning children who were exposed by their parents, and afterwards preserved by others, and educated in a state of servitude, though born free, has been frequently discussed; but I do not find in the constitutions of the princes, my predecessors, any general regulation upon this head extending to all the provinces. There are, indeed, some rescripts of Domitian to Avidius Nigrinus and Armenius Brocchus which ought to be observed, but Bithynia is not comprehended in the provinces therein mentioned. I am of opinion, therefore, that the claims of those who assert their right of freedom upon this footing should be allowed, without obliging them to purchase their liberty by repaying the money advanced for their maintenance. (Bk. X, Letter LXXII.)

QUESTIONS.

1. What source material, that has been lost to us, is mentioned in the above letters? 2. Was Trajan's decision in this matter a wise one? 3. Is modern society, in this respect, better or worse than Roman society?

PLINY TO TRAJAN.

Julius Largus, of Pontus (a person whom I never saw, nor, indeed, ever heard his name till lately), in confidence, Sir, of your distinguishing judgment in my favor, has entrusted me with the execution of the last instance of his loyalty towards you. He has left me, by his will, his estate upon trust, in the first place to receive out of it fifty thousand sesterces* for my own use, and to apply the remainder for the benefit of the cities of Heraclea and Tios, either by erecting some public edifice dedicated to your honor or instituting athletic games, according as I shall judge proper. These games are to be celebrated every five years, and to be called Trojan's games. My principle reason for acquainting you with this bequest is that I may receive your directions which of the respective alternatives to choose. (Bk. X, Letter LXXIX.)

TRAJAN TO PLINY.

By the prudent choice Julius Largus has made of a trustee, one would imagine he had known you perfectly well. You will consider, then, what will most tend to perpetuate his memory, under the circumstances of the respective cities, and make your option accordingly. (Bk. X, Letter LXXX.)

QUESTIONS.

1. Was public spirit entirely lacking in Pliny's day?
2. Was Pliny worthy of the confidence placed in him?
3. Was it a personal or official confidence?

TRAJAN TO PLINY.

You well know, my dearest Secundus, that it is my standing maxim not to create an awe of my person by severe and rigorous measures, and by construing every slight offence into an act of treason; you had no reason, therefore, to hesitate a moment upon the point concerning which you thought proper to consult me. Without entering, therefore, into the merits of that question (to which I would by no means give any attention, though there were ever so many instances of the same kind), I recommend to your care the examination of Dion's accounts relating to the public

---

*Sestertius, about three cents and a half.

works which he has finished, as it is a case in which the interest of the city is concerned, and as Dion neither ought nor, it seems, does, refuse to submit to the examination. (Bk. X, Letter LXXXVI.)

QUESTIONS.

1. What excellent trait does Trajan show in this letter? 2. How does he show his executive ability in his attitude toward Pliny?

PLINY TO TRAJAN.

The free and confederate city of the Amiseni enjoys, by your indulgence, the privilege of its own laws. A memorial being presented to me there, concerning a charitable institution, I have subjoined it to this letter that you may consider, Sir, whether, and how far, this society ought to be licensed or prohibited. (Bk. X, Letter XCIII.)

TRAJAN TO PLINY.

If the petition of the Amiseni which you have transmitted to me, concerning the establishment of a charitable society, be agreeable to their own laws, which by the articles of alliance it is stipulated they shall enjoy, I shall not oppose it, especially if these contributions are employed, not for the purchase of riot and faction, but for the support of the indigent. In other cities, however, which are subject to our laws, I would have all assemblies of this nature prohibited. (Bk. X, Letter XCIV.)

QUESTIONS.

1. Of what previous correspondence are you reminded by these two letters? 2. What relation evidently existed between the Amiseni and the Empire? 3. To what extent was the city free?

PLINY TO TRAJAN.

It is my invariable rule, Sir, to refer to you in all matters where I feel doubtful; for who is more capable of removing my scruples or informing my ignorance? Having never been present at any trials concerning those who profess Christianity, I am unacquainted not only with the nature of their crimes or the measure of their punishment, but how far it is proper to enter into an examination concerning them. Whether, therefore, any difference is usually made with respect to ages, or no distinction is to be observed between the young and the adult; whether repentance entitles them to a pardon, or if a man has once been a Christian it avails nothing to desist from his error; whether the very profession of Christianity, unattended with any criminal act, or only the crimes themselves inherent in the profession are punishable; on all these points I am in great doubt. In the meanwhile the method I have observed towards those who have been brought before me as Christians is this: I asked them whether they were Christians; if they admitted it I repeated the question twice, and threatened them with punishment; if they persisted, I ordered them to be at once punished; for I was persuaded, whatever the nature of their opinions might be, a contumacious and inflexible obstinacy certainly deserved correction. There were others also brought before me possessed with the same infatuation, but, being Roman citizens, I directed them to be sent to Rome. But this crime spreading (as is usually the case) while it was actually under prosecution, several instances of the same nature occurred. An anonymous information was laid before me containing a charge against several persons, who, upon examination, denied they were Christians, or had ever been so. They repeated after me an invocation to the gods and offered religious rites with wine and incense before your statue (which for that purpose I had ordered to be brought, together with those of the gods), and even reviled the name of Christ; whereas there is no forcing, it is said, those who are really Christians into any of these compliances; I thought it proper, therefore, to discharge them. Some among those who were accused by a witness in person at first confessed themseves Christians, but immediately after denied it; the rest owned, indeed, that they had been of that number formerly, but had now (some above three, others more, and a few above twenty years ago) renounced that error. They all worshipped your statue and the images of the gods, uttering imprecations at the same time against the name of Christ. They affirmed the whole of their guilt, or their error, was, that they met on a stated day before it was light and addressed a form of prayer to Christ, as to a divinity, binding themselves by a solemn oath, not for the purposes of any wicked design, but never to commit any fraud, theft, or adultery, never to falsify their word, nor deny a trust when they should be called upon to deliver it up; after which it was their custom to separate, and then reassemble, to eat in common a harmless meal. From this custom, however, they desisted after the publication of my edict, by which, according to your commands, I forbade the meeting of any assembly. After receiving this account, I judged it so much the more necessary to endeavor to extort the real truth by putting two female slaves to the torture who were said to officiate in their religious rites, but all I could discover was evidence of an absurd and extravagant superstition. I deemed it expedient, therefore, to adjourn all further proceedings in order to consult you. For it appears to be a matter highly deserving your consideration, more especially as great numbers must be involved in the danger of these prosecutions, which have already extended, and are still likely to extend, to persons of all ranks and ages, and even of both sexes. In fact, this contagious superstition is not confined to the cities only, but has spread its infection among the neighbouring villages and country. Nevertheless, it still seems possible to restrain its progress. The temples, at least, which were once almost deserted, begin now to be frequented; and the sacred cities, after a long intermission, are again revived; while there is a general demand for the victims, which till lately found very few purchasers. From all this it is easy to conjecture what numbers might be reclaimed if a general pardon were granted to those who shall repent of their error. (Bk. X, Letter XCVII.)

QUESTIONS.

1. Why did Pliny interfere with the Christians? 2. Have you found something similar in other letters? 3. What does he think of their belief? 4. Of their faithfulness? 5. How general is the belief? 6. Why did he not punish them? 7. What was his plan of treatment? 8. Why did he think it would succeed?

TRAJAN TO PLINY.

You have adopted the right course, my dearest Secundus, in investigating the charges against the Christians who were brought before you. It is not possible to lay down any general rule for all such cases. Do not go out of your way to look for them. If, indeed, they should be brought before you, and the crime is proved, they must be punished; with the restriction, however, that where the party denies he is a Christian, and shall make it evident that he is not by invoking our gods, let him (notwithstanding any former suspicion) be pardoned upon his repentance. Anonymous informations ought not to be received in any sort of prosecution. It is introducing a very dangerous precedent, and is quite foreign to the spirit of our age. (Bk. X, Letter XCVIII.)

QUESTIONS.

1. What do you think of the attitude of Trajan toward the Christians?

PLINY TO TRAJAN.

I have hitherto never, Sir, granted an order for post-chaises to any person or upon any occasion, but in affairs that relate to your administration. I find myself, however, at present under a sort of necessity of breaking through this fixed rule. My wife, having received an account of her grandfather's death, and being desirous to wait upon her aunt with all possible expedition, I thought it would be unkind to deny her the use of this privilege, as the grace of so tender an office consists in the early discharge of it, and as I well knew a journey which was founded in filial piety could not fail of your approbation. I should think myself highly ungrateful, therefore, were I not to acknowledge that, among other great obligations which I owe to your indulgence, I have this in particular, that, in confidence of your favor, I have ventured to do, without consulting you, what would have been too late had I waited for your consent. (Bk. X, Letter CXXI.)

TRAJAN TO PLINY.

You did me justice, my dearest Secundus, in confiding in my affection towards you. Without doubt, if you had waited for my consent to forward your wife in her journey by means of those warrants which I have entrusted to your care, the use of them would not have answered your purpose; since it was proper this visit to her aunt should have the additional recommendation of being paid with all possible expedition. (Bk. X, Letter CXXII.)

QUESTIONS.

1. What kind of a relation is shown by these letters to have existed between Trajan and Pliny? 2. What have you seen that indicates to you that Trajan was really a great ruler? 3. Make an outline upon the political condition of a Roman province as shown by Pliny's Letters. 4. How did it differ from the situation under the Republic?

ROMAN LAW.

CHAPTER X.

ROMAN LAW.

Imperatoris Iustiniani Institutionum, Libri Quattuor, with Introductions, Commentary, Excursus, and Translation by J. B. Moyle, B. C. L., M. A. Vol. II. Translation. Oxford (Clarendon Press), 1883.

RANKE asserts (Weltgeschichte, IX, part 2, p. 26) that the Roman Law was the greatest product of the Roman Empire. It is, then, fitting that these studies should close with extracts from the handbook on Roman Law, composed in the time of Justinian, showing the law in its latest form and known as the Institutes of Justinian.

What the Roman Law did for civilization cannot be learned from a simple study of the Law. We must understand that before the Roman lawyers had stripped the laws of their local characteristics there did not exist a body of laws applicable to all civilized peoples. The recognition of the fact that there are common principles underlying all law was a tremendous step in the direction of human unity.

The influence of Roman Law upon later legal development it would be hard to overestimate. Throughout the universities of the continent today the students of law employ the Latin Institutes, together with the Codes and Digest, as in the time of Justinian.

Before the time of Justinian (527 A. D.) there had been three noteworthy attempts at codification: Codex Gregorianus, "a collection mainly of rescripts issued from the time, probably, of Hadrian up to A. D. 284, and principally rescripts of Septimius Severus and the emperors who succeeded him" (date about 300 A. D.); Codex Hermogenianus, "which may be regarded as an appendix to the foregoing" (date probably between 365 and 398 A. D.); Codex Theodosianus (promulgated February, 435 A. D. by Theodosius II.), consisting "of sixteen books, arranged separately in titles and rubrics, and the constitutions in each title were placed in chronological order."

The final codification took place in the time of Justinian.

The first work was to make a single code out of all the codes previously issued, together with the imperial constitutions that had appeared since 439 A. D. The task was undertaken by a commission of ten persons and in April, 529 A. D., the work was published with the name Codex Justinianeus. The older codices were deprived of validity.

The second work prepared was the Pandectae, or Digest, so called because it consisted of a digest of the works of thirty-eight of the most distinguished jurists in Roman history. About one-twentieth part of the material examined went into the new work, that consisted of fifty books or chapters.

These large works were not suited to elementary instruction in law; a text book was necessary. A committee of three men was appointed to produce this work. The result of their labors was the Institutes from which our extracts are taken.

BOOK I.

Title I.

OF JUSTICE AND LAW.

Justice is the set and constant purpose which gives to every man his due. Jurisprudence is the knowledge of things divine and human, the science of the just and the unjust.

Having laid down these general definitions, and our object being the exposition of the law of the Roman people, we think that the most advantageous plan will be to commence with an easy and simple path, and then to proceed to details with a most careful and scrupulous exactness of interpretation. Otherwise, if we begin by burdening the student's memory, as yet weak and untrained, with a multitude and variety of matters, one of two things will happen: we shall either cause him wholly to desert the study of law, or else we shall bring him at last, after great labor, and often, too, distrustful of his own powers (the commonest cause, among the young, of ill success), to a point which he might have reached earlier, without such labor and confident in himself, had he been led along a smoother path.

The precepts of the law are these: to live honestly, to injure no one, and to give every man his due. The study of law consists of two branches, law public, and law private. The former relates to the welfare of the Roman state; the latter to the advantage of the individual citizen. Of private law then we may say that it is of threefold origin, being collected from the precepts of nature, from those of the law of nations, or from those of the civil law of Rome.

QUESTIONS.

1. For whom were the Institutes evidently written? 2. What criticism would you make upon the definition of jurisprudence? 3. Who were the "Roman people" to whom the text refers? 4. What terms do we use to-day as equivalent to "law public and law private"?

TITLE II.

OF THE LAW OF NATURE, THE LAW OF NATIONS, AND THE CIVIL LAW.

The law of nature is that which she has taught all animals; a law not peculiar to the human race, but shared by all living creatures, whether denizens of the air, the dry land, or the sea. Hence comes the union of male and female, which we call marriage; hence the procreation and rearing of children, for this is a law in the knowledge of which we see even the lower animals taking pleasure. The civil law of Rome, and the law of all nations, are thus distinguished. The laws of every people governed by statutes and customs are partly peculiar to itself, partly common to all mankind. Those rules which a state enacts for its own members are peculiar to itself, and are called civil law: those rules prescribed by natural reason for all men are observed by all peoples alike, and are called the law of nations. Thus the laws of the Roman people are partly peculiar to itself, partly common to all nations; a distinction of which we shall take notice as occasion offers. Civil law takes its name from the state wherein it binds; for instance, the civil law of Athens, it being quite correct to speak thus of the enactments of Solon or Draco. So too we call the law observed by the Roman people the civil law of the Romans, or the law of the Quirites; the law, that is to say, which they observe, the Romans being called Quirites after Quirinus. Whenever we speak, however, of civil law, without any qualification, we mean our own; exactly as, when 'the poet' is spoken of, without addition or qualification, the Greeks understand the great Homer, and we understand Vergil. But the law of nations is common to the whole human race; for nations have settled certain things for themselves as occasion and the necessities of human life required. For instance, wars arose, and then followed captivity and slavery, which are contrary to the law of nature; for by the law of nature all men from the beginning were born free. The law of nations again is the source of almost all contracts; for instance, sale, hire, partnership, deposit, loan for consumption, and very many others.

Our law is partly written, partly unwritten, as among the Greeks. The written law consists of statutes, plebiscites, senatusconsults, enactments of the Emperors, edicts of the magistrates, and answers of those learned in the law. A statute is an enactment of the Roman people, which it was wont to make on the motion of a senatorial magistrate, as for instance a consul. A plebiscite is an enactment of commonalty, such as was made on the motion of one of their own magistrates, as a tribune. The commonalty differs from the people as a species from its genus; for 'the people' includes the whole aggregate of citizens, among them patricians and senators, while the term 'commonalty' embraces only such citizens as are not patricians or senators. After the passing however of the statute called the lex Hortensia, plebiscites acquired for the first time the force of statutes. A senatusconsult is a command and ordinance of the senate, for when the Roman people had been so increased that it was difficult to assemble it together for the purpose of creating statutes, it seemed right that the senate should be consulted instead of the people. Again, what the Emperor determines has the force of a statute, the people having conferred on him all their authority and power by the *lex regia*, which was passed concerning his office and authority. Consequently, whatever the Emperor settles by rescript, or decides in his judicial capacity, or ordains by edicts, is clearly a statute: and these are what are called constitutions. Some of these of course are personal, and not to be followed as precedents, since this is not the Emperor's will; for a favour bestowed on individual merit, or a penalty inflicted for individual wrongdoing, or relief given without a precedent, do not go beyond the particular person: though others are general, and bind all beyond a doubt. The edicts of the praetors too have no small legal authority, and these we are used to call the *jus honorarium*, because those who occupy posts of honour in the state, in other words the magistrates, have given authority to this branch of law. The curule aediles also used to issue an edict relating to certain matters, which forms part of the *jus honorarium*. The answers of those learned in the law are the opinions and views of persons authorised to determine and expound the law; for it was of old provided that certain persons should publicly interpret the laws, who were called jurisconsults, and whom the Emperor privileged to give formal answers. If they were unanimous the judge was forbidden by imperial constitution to depart from their opinion, so great was its authority. The unwritten law is that which usage has approved: for ancient customs, when approved by consent of those who follow them, are like statute. And this division of the civil law into two kinds seems not inappropriate, for it appears to have originated in the institutions of two states, namely Athens and Lacedaemon; it having been usual in the latter to commit to memory what was observed as law, while the Athenians observed only what they had expressed in written statutes.

But the laws of nature, which are observed by all nations alike, are established, as it were, by divine providence, and remain ever fixed and immutable: but the municipal laws of each individual state are subject to frequent change, either by the tacit consent of the people, or by the subsequent enactment of another statute. The whole of the law which we observe relates either to persons, or to things, or to actions. And first let us speak of persons: for it is useless to know the law without knowing the persons for whose sake it was established.

QUESTIONS.

1. Was the "Law of Nature" a law in the same sense that the "Civil Law" was? 2. Did the "Law of Nations" exist as a distinct body of law? 3. What relation between this Roman conception of the "Law of Nations" and the permanent value of the Institutes? 4. Does the term "Civil Law" mean the same thing to us as to the writer of the Institutes? 5. What sentence anticipating the Declaration of Independence do you find here? 6. Of what period in the history of Rome would the "plepiscites" be characteristic? The "Senatusconsults"? The "Enactments of the Emperors"? 7. Show that the Roman Law was the product of time. 8. What was peculiar about the position of the judge in the Roman system? 9. Have we both written and unwritten law?

TITLE III.

OF THE LAW OF PERSONS.

In the law of persons, then, the first division is into free men and slaves. Freedom, from which men are called free, is a man's natural power of doing what he pleases, so far as he is not prevented by force or law: slavery is an institution of the law of nations, against nature subjecting one man to the dominion of another. The name 'slave' is derived from the practice of generals to order the preservation and sale of captives, instead of killing them; hence they are also called *mancipia*, because they are taken from the enemy by the strong hand. Slaves are either born so, their mothers being slaves themselves; or they become so, and this either by the law of nations, that is to say by capture in war, or by the civil law, as when a free man, over twenty years of age, collusively allows himself to be sold in order that he may share the purchase money. The condition of all slaves is one and the same: in the conditions of free men there are many distinctions; to begin with, they are either free born, or made free.

QUESTIONS.

1. Would our definition of "freedom" differ from the Roman's? 2. How was slavery a good thing when first introduced? 3. Point out all the ways in which our laws differ from the laws included in Title III. 4. What do we do with our prisoners? 5. Why did not the Romans take the same attitude toward slavery that we take to-day?

TITLE IV.

OF MEN FREE BORN.

A free born man is one free from his birth, being the offspring of parents united in wedlock, whether both be freeborn or both made free, or one made free and the other freeborn. He is also freeborn if his mother be free, even though his father be a slave.

QUESTIONS.

1. Name all the different combinations by which a child might be freeborn. 2. Did the Roman Law favor the acquisition of freedom?

TITLE V.

OF FREEDMEN.

Those are freedmen, or made free, who have been manumitted from legal slavery. Manumission is the giving of freedom; for while a man is in slavery he is subject to the power once known as *manus;* and from that power he is set free by manumission. All this originated in the law of nations; for by natural law all men were born free—slavery, and by consequence manumission, being unknown. But afterwards slavery came in by the law of nations, and was followed by the boon of manumission; so that though we are all known by the common name of 'man,' three classes of men came into existence with the law of nations, namely men free born, slaves, and thirdly freedmen who had ceased to be slaves. Manumission may take place in various ways: either in the holy church, according to the sacred constitutions, or by default in a fictitious vindication, or before friends, or by letter, or by testament or any other expression of a man's last will: and indeed there are many other modes in which freedom may be acquired, introduced by the constitutions of earlier emperors as well as by our own. It is usual for slaves to be manumitted by their masters at any time, even when the magistrate is merely passing by, as for instance while the praetor or proconsul or governor of a province is going to the baths or the theater.

Of freedmen there were formerly three grades; for those who were manumitted sometimes obtained a higher freedom fully recognized by the laws, and became Roman citizens; sometimes a lower form, becoming by the lex Junia Norbana Latins; and sometimes finally a liberty still more circumscribed, being placed by the lex Aelia Sentia on the footing of enemies surrendered at discretion. This last and lowest class however has long ceased to exist, and the title of Latin also had become rare: and so in our goodness, which desires to raise and improve in every matter, we have amended this in two constitutions, and reintroduced the earlier usage; for in the earliest infancy of Rome there was but one simple type of liberty, namely that possessed by the manumitter, the only distinction possible being that the latter was freeborn, while the manumitted slave became a freedman. We have abolished the class of *dediticci*, or enemies surrendered at discretion, by our constitution, published among those our decisions, by which, at the suggestion of the eminent Tribonian, our quaestor, we have set at rest the disputes of the older law. By another constitution, which shines brightly among the imperial enactments, and suggested by the same quaestor, we have altered the position of the *Latini Juniani*, and dispensed with all the rules relating to their condition; and have endowed with the citizenship of Rome all freedmen alike, without regard to the age of the person manumitted, the nature of the master's ownership, or the mode of manumission, in accordance with the earlier usage; with the addition of many new modes in which freedom coupled with the Roman citizenship, the only kind of freedom now known, may be bestowed on slaves.

QUESTIONS.

1. What was the difference between a "freeman" and a "freedman"? 2. Was "manumission" a common thing in the Empire? 3. Did the laws favor it? 4. In what way was the position of the freedman better under the Empire than under the Republic? 5. What would be the effect of imperial legislation upon "equality before the law"?

TITLE VI.

OF PERSONS UNABLE TO MANUMIT, AND THE CAUSES OF THEIR INCAPACITY.

In some cases however manumission is not permitted; for an owner who would defraud his creditors by an intended manumission attempts in vain to manumit, the act being declared void by the lex Aelia Sentia. A master however who is insolvent may institute one of his slaves heir in his will, conferring freedom on him at the same time, so that he may become free and his sole and necessary heir, provided no one else takes as heir under the will, either because no one else was instituted at all, or because the person instituted for some reason or other does not take the inheritance. And this was a judicious provision of the lex Aelia Sentia, for it was most desirable that persons in embarrassed circumstances, who could get no other heir, should have a slave as necessary heir to satisfy their creditors' claims, or at least (if he did not do this) the creditors might sell the estate in the slave's name, so as to save the memory of the deceased from disrepute. The law is the same if the slave be instituted heir without liberty being expressly given him, this being enacted by our constitution in all cases, and not merely where the master is insolvent; so that in accordance with the modern spirit of humanity, institution will be equivalent to a gift of liberty; for it is unlikely, in spite of the omission of the grant of freedom, that one should have wished the person whom one has chosen as one's heir to remain a slave, so that one should have no heir at all. If a person is insolvent at the time of manumission, or becomes so by the manumission itself, this is manumission in fraud of creditors. It is however now settled law, that the gift of liberty is not avoided unless the intention of the manumitter was fraudulent, even though his property is in fact insufficient to meet his creditor's claims; for men often hope and believe that they are better off than they really are. Consequently, we understand a gift of liberty to be avoided only when the creditors are defrauded both by the intention of the manumitter, and in fact: that is to say, by his property being insufficient to meet their claims.

The same lex Aelia Sentia makes it unlawful for a master under twenty years of age to manumit, except in the mode of fictitious vindication, preceded by proof of some legitimate motive before the council. It is a legitimate motive of manumission if the slave to be manumitted be, for instance, the father or mother of the manumitter, or his son or daughter, or his natural mother or sister, his teacher or governor, his nurse or foster-brother, or a slave whom he wishes to make his agent, or a female slave whom he intends to marry; provided he marry her within six months, and provided that the slave intended as an agent is not less than seventeen years of age at the time of manumission. When a motive for manumission, whether true or false, has once been proved, the council cannot withdraw its sanction.

Thus the lex Aelia Sentia having prescribed a certain mode of manumission for owners under twenty, it followed that though a person fourteen years of age could make a will, and therein institute an heir and leave legacies, yet he could not confer liberty on a slave until he had completed his twentieth year. But it seemed an intolerable hardship that a man who had the power of disposing freely of all his property by will should not be allowed to give his freedom to a single slave: wherefore we allow him to deal in his last will as he pleases with his slaves as with the rest of his property, and even to give them their liberty if he will. But liberty being a boon beyond price, for which very reason the power of manumission was denied by the older law to owners under twenty years of age, we have as it were selected a middle course, and permitted persons under twenty years of age to manumit their slaves by will, but not until they have completed their seventeenth and entered on their eighteenth year. For when ancient custom allowed persons of this age to plead on behalf of others, why should not their judgment be deemed sound enough to enable them to use discretion in giving freedom to their own slaves?

QUESTIONS.

1. The Roman Law has been called "written reason." Prove from the above extract that it is justly so called. 2. Was the spirit of the Roman Law favorable or unfavorable to slavery? 3. How could the "father of the manumitter" be a slave? 4. Did economic reasons ever stand in the way of manumission? 5. Why was manumission a more natural thing in the Empire than in this country before the war?

TITLE VII.

OF THE REPEAL OF THE LEX FUFIA CANINIA.

Moreover, by the lex Fufia Caninia a limit was placed on the number of slaves who could receive testamentary manumission: but this law we have thought fit to repeal, as an obstacle to freedom and to some extent invidious, for it was certainly inhuman to take away from a man on his deathbed the right of liberating the whole of his slaves, which he could have exercised at any moment during his lifetime, unless there were some other obstacle to the act of manumission.

QUESTIONS.

1. How is the liberality of the Empire shown? 2. How the reasonableness of the Roman Law? 3. How the tendency toward equality?

TITLE VIII.

OF PERSONS INDEPENDENT OR DEPENDENT.

Another division of the law relating to persons classifies them as either independent or dependent. Those again who are dependent are in the power either of parents or of masters. Let us first then consider those who are dependent, for by learning who these are we shall at the same time learn who are independent. And first let us look at those who are in the power of masters.

Now slaves are in the power of masters, a power recognized by the law of all nations, for all nations present the spectacle of masters invested with power of life and death over slaves; and to whatever is acquired through a slave his owner is entitled. But in the present day no one under our sway is permitted to indulge in excessive harshness towards his slaves, without some reason recognized by law; for, by a constitution of the Emperor Pius Antoninus, a man is made as liable to punishment for killing his own slave as for killing the slave of another person; and extreme severity on the part of masters is checked by another constitution whereby the same Emperor, in answer to enquiries from presidents of provinces concerning slaves who take refuge at churches or statues of the Emperor, commanded that on proof of intolerable cruelty a master should be compelled to sell his slaves on fair terms, so as to receive their value. And both of these are reasonable enactments, for the public interest requires that no one should make an evil use of his own property. The terms of the rescript of Antoninus to Aelius Marcianus are as follows:—'The powers of masters over their slaves ought to continue undiminished, nor ought any man to be deprived of his lawful rights; but it is the master's own interest that relief justly sought against cruelty, insufficient sustenance, or intolerable wrong, should not be denied. I enjoin you then to look into the complaints of the slaves of Julius Sabinus, who have fled for protection to the statue of the Emperor, and if you find them treated with undue harshness or other ignominious wrong, order them to be sold, so that they may not again fall under the power of their master; and the latter will find if he attempts to evade this my enactment, I shall visit his offence with severe punishment.'

QUESTIONS.

1. How did the position of a man's slaves differ from that of his cattle? 2. What checks were exercised by the state upon the exercise of the master's authority? 3. On what ground was this done? 4. Why did the slaves "flee to the statue of the Emperor"?

TITLE IX.

OF PATERNAL POWER.

Our children whom we have begotten in lawful wedlock are in our power. Wedlock or matrimony is the union of male and female, involving the habitual intercourse of daily life. The power which we have over our children is peculiar to Roman citizens and is found in no other nation. The offspring then of you and your wife is in your power, and so too is that of your son and his wife, that is to say, your grandson and granddaughter, and so on. But the offspring of your daughter is not in your power, but in that of its own father.

QUESTIONS.

1. What was there peculiar about the Roman paternal power? 2. Why was not the offspring of a man's daughter in his power? 3. Was his married daughter in his power? 4. How does our family organization differ from that of the Roman? 5. Which is superior, and why?

BOOK II.

TITLE I.

OF THE DIFFERENT KINDS OF THINGS.

In the preceding book we have expounded the law of Persons: now let us proceed to the law of Things. Of these some admit of private ownership, while others, it is held, cannot belong to individuals: for some things are by natural law common to all, some are public, some belong to a society or corporation, and some belong to no one. But most things belong to individuals, being acquired by various titles, as will appear from what follows.

QUESTIONS.

1. How many divisions of things do the Institutes make? 2. Do those divisions exist in modern society?

THINGS COMMON TO ALL.

Thus, the following things are by natural law common to all—the air, running water, the sea, and consequently the sea-shore. No one therefore is forbidden access to the sea-shore, provided he abstains from injury to houses, monuments, and buildings generally; for these are not, like the sea itself, subject to the law of nations. On the other hand, all rivers and harbours are public, so that all persons have a right to fish therein. The sea-shore extends to the limit of the highest tide in time of storm or winter. Again, the public use of the banks of a river, as of the river itself, is part of the law of nations; consequently every one is entitled to bring his vessel to the bank, and fasten cables to the trees growing there, and use it as a resting place for the cargo, as freely as he may navigate the river itself. But the ownership of the bank is in the owner of the adjoining land, and consequently so too is the ownership of the trees which grow upon it. Again, the public use of the sea-shore, as of the sea itself, is part of the law of nations; consequently everyone is free to build a cottage upon it for purposes of retreat, as well as to dry his nets and haul them up from the sea. But they cannot be said to belong to anyone as private property, but rather are subject to the same law as the sea itself, with the soil or sand which lies beneath it. As examples of things belonging to a society or corporation, and not to individuals, may be cited buildings in cities—theaters, racecourses, and such other similar things as belong to cities in their corporate capacity.

QUESTIONS.

1. To what extent does our modern law agree with the Roman Law contained in the above paragraph?

SACRED THINGS.

Things which are sacred, devoted to superstitious uses, or sanctioned, belong to no one, for what is subject to divine law is no one's property. Those things are sacred which have been duly consecrated to God by His ministers, such as churches and votive offerings which have been properly dedicated to His service; and these we have by our constitution forbidden to be alienated or pledged, except to redeem captives from bondage. If any one attempts to consecrate a thing for himself and by his own authority, its character is unaltered, and it does not become sacred. The ground on which a sacred building is erected remains sacred even after the destruction of the building, as was declared also by Papinian. Any one can devote a place to superstitious uses of his own free will, that is to say, by burying a dead body in his own land. It is not lawful however to bury in land which one owns jointly with some one else, or which has not hitherto been used for this purpose, without the other's consent, though one may lawfully bury in a common sepulchre even without such consent. Again, the owner may not devote a place to superstitious uses in which another has a usufruct without the consent of the latter. It is lawful to bury in another man's ground if he gives permission, and the ground thereby becomes religious even though he should not give his consent to the interment till after it has taken place. Sanctioned things too, such as city walls and gates, are, in a sense, subject to divine law, and therefore are not owned by any individual. Such walls are said to be 'sanctioned,' because any offence against them is visited with capital punishment; for which reason those parts of the laws in which we establish a penalty for their transgressors are called sanctions.

QUESTIONS.

1. Is our law touching "sacred things" the same as the Roman? 2. May church edifices be alienated today? 3. Why was the one exception made in the Institutes? 4. Does any such respect for sacred ground exist in our laws? 5. Why should walls and gates be sacred?

HOW THINGS BECOME PRIVATE PROPERTY.

Things become the private property of individuals in many ways, for the titles by which we acquire ownership in them are some of them titles of natural law, which, as we said, is called the law of nations, while some of them are titles of civil law. It will thus be more convenient to take the older law first: and natural law is clearly the older, having been instituted by nature at the first origin of mankind, whereas civil laws first came into existence when states began to be founded, magistrates to be created, and laws to be written.

Wild animals, birds, and fish, that is to say all the creatures which the land, the sea, and the sky produce, as soon as they are caught by any one become at once the property of their captor by the law of nations; for natural reason admits the title of the first occupant to that which previously had no owner. So far as the occupant's title is concerned, it is immaterial whether it is on his own land or on that of another that he catches wild animals or birds, though it is clear that if he goes on another man's land for the sake of hunting or fowling, the later may forbid him entry if aware of his purpose. An animal thus caught by you is deemed your property so long as it is completely under your control; but so soon as it has escaped from your control, and recovered its natural liberty, it ceases to be yours, and belongs to the first person who subsequently catches it. It is deemed to have recovered its natural liberty when you have lost sight of it, or when, though it is still in your sight, it would be difficult to pursue it. It has been doubted whether a wild animal becomes your property immediately you have wounded it so severely as to be able to catch it. Some have thought that it becomes yours at once, and remains so long as you pursue it, though it ceases to be yours when you cease the pursuit, and becomes again the property of any one who catches it: others have been of the opinion that it does not belong to you till you have actually caught it. And we confirm this latter view, for it may happen in many ways that you will not capture it. Bees again are naturally wild; hence if a swarm settles on your tree, it is no more considered yours, until you have hived it, than the birds which build their nests there, and consequently if it is hived by someone else, it becomes his property. So too any one may take the honeycombs which bees may chance to have made, though, of course, if you see some one coming on your land for this purpose, you have a right to forbid him entry before that purpose is affected. A swarm which has flown from your hive is considered to remain yours so long as it is in your sight and easy of pursuit: otherwise it belongs to the first person who catches it. Pea-fowl too and pigeons are naturally wild, and it is no valid objection that they are used to return to the same spots from which they fly away, for bees do this; and it is admitted that bees are wild by nature; and some people have deer so tame that they will go into the woods and yet habitually come back again, and still no one denies that they are naturally wild. With regard, however, to animals which have this habit of going away and coming back again, the rule has been established that they are deemed yours so long as they have the intent to return: for if they cease to have this intention they cease to be yours, and belong to the first person who takes them; and when they lose the habit they seem also to have lost the intention of returning. Fowls and geese are not naturally wild, as is shown by the fact that there are some kinds of fowls and geese which we call wild kinds. Hence if your geese and fowls are frightened and fly away they are considered to continue yours wherever they may be, even though you have lost sight of them; and any one who keeps them intending thereby to make a profit is held guilty of theft. Things again which we capture from the enemy at once becomes ours by the law of nations, so that by this rule, even free men become our slaves, though, if they escape from our power and return to their own people, they recover their previous condition. Precious stones, too, and gems, and all other things found on the seashore, become immediately by natural law the property of the finder: and by the same law the young of animals of which you are the owner become your property also.

QUESTIONS.

1. Are the generalizations in the first paragraph above correct? 2. How do our game laws differ from the Roman? 3. Which is the more advanced? 4. How are the Roman laws dealing with bees inferior to ours? 5. What do you think about the reasoning upon fowls and geese? 6. What is our law touching property found on the seashore?

OWNERSHIP OF LAND.

Moreover, soil which a river has added to your land by alluvion becomes yours by the law of nations. Alluvion is an imperceptible addition; and that which is added so gradually that you cannot perceive the exact increase from one moment of time to another is added by alluvion. If, however, the violence of a stream sweeps away a parcel of your land and carries it down to the land of your neighbor, it clearly remains yours; though, of course, if in process of time it becomes firmly attached to your neighbor's land, and the trees which it carried with it strike root in the latter, they are deemed from that time to have become part and parcel thereof. When an island rises in the sea, though this rarely happens, it belongs to the first occupant; for, until occupied, it is held to belong to no one. If, however (as often occurs), an island rises in a river, and it lies in the middle of the stream, it belongs in common to the landholders on either bank, in proportion to the extent of their riparian interest; but if it lies nearer to one bank than to the other, it belongs to the landowners on that bank only. If a river divides into two channels, and by uniting again these channels transform a man's land into an island, the ownership of that land is in no way altered: but if a river entirely leaves its old channel and begins to run in a new one the old channel belongs to the landowners on either side of it in proportion to the extent of their riparian interest, while the new one acquires the same legal character as the river itself, and becomes public. But if after a while the river returns to its old channel the new channel again becomes the property of those who possess the land along its banks. It is otherwise if one's land is wholly flooded, for a flood does not permanently alter the nature of the land. and consequently if the water goes back the soil clearly belongs to its previous owners.

QUESTIONS.

1. Make a list of all the legal questions dealt with in the last paragraph and show the reasonableness of the Roman Law. 2. Prepare an outline indicating all of the Roman Law that still holds good and all that has been abandoned and show why it has been abandoned.

EUROPEAN HISTORY STUDIES.

FRED MORROW FLING, PH.D.,
Professor of European History, University of Nebraska.

EDITOR.

A monthly publication. Subscription 40 cents. Extracts from the sources; translations from the writers of the period studied.

Vol. III. The French Revolution.

No.	I. Sept.,	1899.	Absolutism in the Church: The Constitution.
No.	II. Oct.,	1899.	Struggle against Absolutism in the Church; Certificates of Confession.
No.	III. Nov.,	1899.	The Church and the Philosophers.
No.	IV. Dec.,	1899.	Reform Edicts; Turgot.
No.	V. Jan.,	1900.	The Administration of Finance; Necker.
No.	VI. Feb.,	1900.	The Notables.
No.	VII. March,	1900.	The King and the Parliaments.
No.	VIII. April,	1900.	The Age of Pamphlets.
No.	IX. May,	19.0.	The Elections to the States General.
No.	X. June,	1900.	The Cahiers of Complaints.

Vol. II. Civilization of the Middle Ages.

1898-1899. No. I. Christian and Pagan. No. II. The Teutonic Barbarians. No. III. Selections from the Koran. No. IV. Chivalry and the Mode of Warfare. No. V. Feudalism. No. VI. Monasticism. No. VII. The Jews of Angevin England. No. VIII. Rise of Cities. No. IX. The Trades of Paris. No. X. Mediaeval Science.
Bound in cloth, 60 cents; for introduction, 50 cents net.

Vol. I. Greek and Roman Civilization.

1897-1898. No. I. The Homeric Age. No. II. The Athenian Constitution. No. III. Spartan Life. No. IV. Alexander's Mode of Warfare. No. V. The Achaen League. No. VI. Roman Constitution No. VII. Roman Life of the First Punic War. No. VIII. Roman Life of the Jugurthine Period. No. IX. Roman Life Under the Empire. No. X. Roman Laws.
Bound in cloth, 60 cents; for introduction, 50 cents net.

BOOKS ON METHOD

Studies in European and American History.
F. M. FLING AND H. W. CALDWELL.

A book of over 300 pages setting forth the principles, methods, and advantages of the "Source Method." Containing also studies on such subjects as The Grecian Period, The Romans, Absolute Monarchies, The French Revolution, Early Virginia History, Early Massachusetts Laws, and others. Cloth. Price, $1.00.

Outlines of Historical Method.
F. M. FLING, PH.D.

This volume contains some of the strongest papers yet published in English on Method in History. It treats clearly the subjects of External and Internal Criticism of Sources and Synthetic Operations. Cloth. Price, 60 cents.

The Leaflets

All the Leaflets named above are kept in stock. Single copy, 5 cents each. Ten or more copies of one number, 4 cents each. Ten or more subscriptions to the current volume, or ten or more sets of any previous volume unbound, sent to one address at 30 cents each. Samples of the Leaflets sent free to any address.

ADDRESS J. H. MILLER, PUBLISHER, LINCON, NEB.

AMERICAN HISTORY STUDIES.

H. W. CALDWELL, A. M.,

Professor of American History, University of Nebraska.

EDITOR.

A monthly publication. Subscription 40 cents. Extracts from the sources of American History, Early Laws, Treaties, State Papers, Letters, Speeches, etc

Vol. III. Territorial Development: Expansion.

No. I. Sept., 1899. Territorial Boundaries.
No. II. Oct., 1899. First National Boundaries.
No. III. Nov., 1899. The Northwest Territory.
No. IV. Dec., 1899. Acquisition of Louisiana.
No. V. Jan., 1900. Purchase of Florida.
No. VI. Feb., 1900. Annexation of Texas.
No. VII. March, 1900. Conquest of California and New Mexico
No. VIII. April, 1900. " "
No. IX. May, 1900. Alaska and Hawaii.
No. X. June, 19.0. West Indies and the Philippines.

Vol. II. Some American Legislators.

1898-1899. No. I. Gallatin. No. II. J. Q Adams. No. III. Clay. No. IV. Webster. No. V. Calhoun. No. VI. Sumner. No. VII. Douglas. No. VIII. Seward. No. IX. Chase No. X. Blaine.

Vol. I. A Survey of American History.

1897-1898. No. I. Founding of the Colonies. No. II Development of Union among the Colonies. No. III. Cause of the Revolution. No. IV. Formation of the Constitution. No. V. Growth of Nationality. No. VI. Slavery (1). No. VII. Slavery (2). No. VIII Civil War and Reconstruction. No. IX. Foreign Relations. No. X. Industrial Development. [Extra. Early Colonial Laws, 5 cents.]

BOOKS ON METHOD

Studies in European and American History.

F. M. FLING AND H. W. CALDWELL.

A book of over 300 pages setting forth the principles, methods, and advantages of the "Source Method." Containing also studies on such subjects as The Grecian Period, The Romans, Absolute Monarchies, The French Revolution, Early Virginia History Early Massachusetts Laws, and others. Cloth. Price, $1 00.

Outlines of Historical Method.

F. M. FLING, PH.D.

This volume contains some of the strongest papers yet published in English on Method in History. It treats clearly the subjects of External and Internal Criticism of Sources and Synthetic Operations. Cloth. Price, 60 cents.

The Leaflets

All the Leaflets named above are kept in stock. Single copy, 5 cents each. Ten or more copies of one number, 4 cents each. Ten or more subscriptions to the current volume, or ten or more sets of any previous volume unbound, sent to one address at 30 cents each. Samples of the Leaflets sent free to any address.

ADDRESS J. H. MILLER, PUBLISHER, LINCON, NEB.